The Tramways of South Yorkshire and Humberside

Reprinted from **Great British Tramway Networks**

At the peak of its development, in 1927, the British tramway industry employed 14,481 cars working on 2,554 miles of route. Every large and medium-sized town had its tramway system, usually municipally-operated, and in other populated areas such as the major coalfields there were often interurban tramways operated by companies. The company and municipal tramways together formed considerable networks of lines, and one such network was to be found in South Yorkshire, where in the mid-1920s it was possible to travel by electric tramcar from Barnsley through the Dearne Valley and the outskirts of Swinton to Rawmarsh, Rotherham and Sheffield, changing cars three times on the way. All the tramways in South Yorkshire and Humberside were built to the standard 4ft. 8½in. gauge, so there were no problems of differing gauges as there were in some other parts of Britain.

The first tramway undertaking to be encountered by anyone making this journey was that of the Barnsley and District Electric Traction Co. Ltd., whose route, starting at Smithies near Monk Bretton Colliery, ran through the centre of Barnsley to a point about two miles beyond, there forking into branches terminating at Worsborough Bridge and Worsborough Dale. This company was a local subsidiary of the British Electric Traction Co. Ltd., and had 13 four-wheel double-deck cars and one demi-car. The service was inaugurated at the end of 1902, under powers granted to the B.E.T. itself in 1900, the Barnsley company not being formed until 1902. Earlier, in 1898, there had been talk of three other companies applying for local tramway powers, and Barnsley Corporation did apply in 1900 for powers for a much more ambitious route network than the B.E.T. scheme. All these early proposals, including the B.E.T., were for 3ft. 6in. gauge lines, but as eventually built the Barnsley tramways were of 4ft. 8½in. gauge.

COVER PHOTOGRAPH **Sheffield 510, 513 and 501 in Queen's Road on a special tour during the last week of tramway operation in October, 1960.**

J. M. Davis

Four short extensions were proposed, but withdrawn or rejected and not built. These were along Park Road, along Dodworth Road, along Huddersfield Road, and further along the Wakefield Road beyond Smithies. Opposition by the Great Central Railway Company to a tramway level crossing at Worsborough Bridge prevented the construction of a very much longer authorised extension from there through Birdwell and Hoyland Common to Hoyland Nether. In 1913 the company began running motor buses to Hoyland and other points, and in 1919 "Electric" was dropped from the title. The Barnsley company changed its name in 1928 to Yorkshire Traction Co. Ltd. (known by most of the local people as "Tracky") and abandoned the tramways in 1930, having already grown into a large bus operator. The Y.T.C. became, and still is, the largest bus company in Britain to have originated as a tramway company, except for Bristol and City of Oxford.

At a road junction just south of Barnsley Market Place the left fork was occupied by a dead-end terminal of the Dearne District Light Railways, and although the metals of the two systems were only a few feet apart, and both of standard gauge, no points were ever laid to make a connection. The D.D.L.R. Joint Committee, comprising the four Urban District Councils of Wombwell, Wath-upon-Dearne, Bolton-upon-Dearne and Thurnscoe, was authorised in 1915 to construct 15¼ miles of tramway linking Barnsley with Wath and elsewhere, but did not open its route until 1924. This was the last complete street tramway system to be inaugurated in the British Isles, and actually started after the Sheerness and Taunton electric tramways had been completely abandoned, and only three months before two more were to follow. Severe bus competition from the Barnsley and District company, which was already working on the route concerned, existed right from the start. Local councillors had hoped to divert traffic from the buses to the new municipal enterprise, but unfortunately they did not succeed, and after making heavy financial losses the trams were abandoned only nine years later, in 1933, in favour of additional Barnsley (now Yorkshire Traction) buses.

Leaving Barnsley, the D.D.L.R. passed through Stairfoot, Wombwell and West Melton to Wath-upon-Dearne, where there was a three-way junction. To the left a tortuous route, served by the through cars from Barnsley, wound its way through Bolton-upon-Dearne and Goldthorpe to Thurnscoe, with reserved track through Bolton cutting and a quarry; straight ahead was the heavy industrial district of Manvers Main; and to the right a line led to the Woodman Inn, Swinton, these two being worked as separate shuttle services. The D.D.L.R. had originally hoped to continue from Manvers Main to Mexborough, in which case the Thurnscoe line would have joined the main route at Manvers Main instead of Wath. But it was again the opposition of the Great Central Railway over a level crossing that forced the D.D.L.R. to terminate at Manvers Main Colliery.

The entire Dearne District line was single track, with passing loops, and because of the likelihood of mining subsidence the tracks were laid on sleepers, but as most of them were paved over this was not visible. Bad planning hampered the trams in competing with the rival bus company, for some passing loops were at the wrong places, so that trams often had to wait for each other much longer than should have been the case. The rolling stock was very good, comprising thirty up-to-date long-wheelbase single-deckers with front exits, and after the closure of the D.D.L.R. nine had a new lease of life on the tramway systems of Lytham St. Annes and Falkirk. An unusual feature was the use of the American term "Car Barns" as the official title and postal address of the tram depot at Wombwell.

The next link in the chain of tramways was the undertaking of the Mexborough and Swinton Tramways Company, a subsidiary of the National Electric Construction Co. Ltd., which owned the tramway companies at Mexborough, Oxford, Rhondda and Torquay and itself ran the Dewsbury and Ossett tramway. The Mexborough company worked a standard-gauge tramway from the Rotherham boundary through Rawmarsh, Swinton and Mexborough to the Old Toll Bar at Denaby. In 1915 the company inaugurated two early pioneer trolleybus routes. One ran from Mexborough town centre to Manvers Main, where it was almost met nine years later by the Dearne District trams; the two termini were a quarter-mile apart, but Manvers Main was nonetheless the only place in Great Britain to have trolleybuses before it had a tramway. The other 1915 route was from the Old Toll Bar to Conisbrough, only two miles from the Doncaster Corporation tramways at Warmsworth. The Dearne District branch to the Woodman Inn, Swinton, already mentioned, made a triangular junction with the Mexborough lines at this point, but it appears that the only through service ever worked was on just three Saturdays during 1928, from West Melton to Rotherham.

When first opened in 1907, the Mexborough and Swinton tramway was worked on the Dolter surface-contact system, but was converted in the following year to overhead trolley. Systems of this type, though none proved very successful, were adopted in several towns in the early days, when there was a good deal of prejudice against overhead wires on the score of unsightliness. Current was supplied from metal studs placed at intervals between the rails, and these became live only when energised by a magnetic skate under the car. This completed the circuit by operating a contact inside the stud, which supposedly became dead again after the car had passed. At Mexborough the studs repeatedly remained "live" and the Board of Trade eventually ordered operation to cease, leaving Swinton without a tram service until the overhead was completed some weeks later.

The tramway passed beneath two low railway bridges, at Rawmarsh and Swinton, and the Mexborough trams (and those used for a through joint service by Rotherham Corporation) were fitted with low-height top covers. In 1928-29 the Mexborough and Swinton Tramways Company (Traction Company from 1929) replaced its 20 trams with a fleet of single-deck trolleybuses, and in 1931 the National Electric Construction Co. Ltd. became part of the British Electric Traction group. The trolleybus fleet later grew to 39 units, but was itself replaced by lowbridge double-deck motor buses in 1961. Operations were taken over by the Yorkshire Traction Co. Ltd. eight years later.

At Rotherham Bridge, the Mexborough lines connected with those of Rotherham Corporation, and company trams ran through to this town. Rotherham had six tram routes, of which four (Rawmarsh Road, Broom Road, Kimberworth and Thrybergh) were replaced by trolleybuses in 1929-31, and one (Canklow) by motor buses in 1934. A trolleybus extension from Broom Top, via Wickersley and Bramley to Maltby, only the third in the whole of Great Britain, was opened as long ago as 1912, and from 1924 these vehicles ran through to the town centre alongside the Broom Road trams. Other trolleybus routes were opened later to Greasbrough and to Silverwood Colliery. Until 1955 the Rotherham trolleybus fleet was wholly single-decked, but in the following years 20 of these vehicles were given new double-deck bodies, and 23 others were sold for further service in Spain. The last Rotherham trolleybuses were withdrawn in 1965.

The sixth tram route ran from Rotherham Centre to the Sheffield boundary at Templeborough, and in 1933, when its future was carefully considered, it was decided to reconstruct the track and continue operations, so as not to interfere with the joint through service to Sheffield. In addition a fleet of eleven brand-new cars was purchased, being specially designed for the Rotherham—Sheffield service, both of whose termini were loops; hence these trams were single-ended, the only cars in England built new in this form. They had only one entrance and staircase, and as the seats were not reversible they were made very comfortable, those at the front of the top deck being faced by a sloping windscreen. The complete tram, in fact, had exactly the appearance, inside and out, of a trolleybus running on flanged wheels.

A new reversing triangle was laid at Templeborough, to enable the single-ended cars to provide short workings to this point, and, thus reprieved and rejuvenated at the eleventh hour, this part of the Rotherham tramways continued to serve the public for another 15 years until the reconstruction of a bridge at Tinsley caused trams to be withdrawn from the central portion of the route in 1948. (This section, from Tinsley to Templeborough, had been owned by Rotherham Corporation until sold in 1926 to Sheffield.) Rotherham trams continued to work as far as Templeborough for a few months, but operation finally ceased in 1949. Incidentally, in 1940 the Rotherham to Templeborough route had been equipped with trolleybus wires to provide through trolleybus services across the town to the several steel-works, but these proved a failure in competition with the trams, and were discontinued.

The tramway from Rotherham to Sheffield passed through Great Britain's principal steel-making area, with several miles of continuous factories and very heavy industry, on which at its busiest period this tram route had to provide an intensely frequent service with a constant procession of fully-loaded cars, and workmen's through services across Sheffield to most of the far suburbs. At Rotherham itself, John Baker and Bessemer Ltd., and also Steel Peech and Tozer Ltd., produced huge quantities of tramcar wheels, tyres and axles. On the section through Templeborough and Tinsley, there are the East Hecla Works of Hadfields Ltd., and the Imperial Works of Edgar Allen & Co. Ltd., whilst in Rutland Road, a little to the north of Sheffield

A 62-ton "Grand Union" tramway junction for Salford Corporation laid out in Hadfields yard at Sheffield early in 1936.

(Hadfields Ltd.

city centre, was the home of Samuel Osborn & Co. Ltd., the makers of Osborn's Titan Manganese Steel. All three of these firms became world-famous for the production of special tramway trackwork for complicated junctions and depot entrances; their names could be seen on almost every tramway junction and crossing in Britain, and in many countries abroad, not to mention their vast contribution to railway permanent way as well. All three firms still survive today, with minor changes to their names, and making other special steel products.

Sheffield, as befits the steel metropolis, had a large and very progressive tramway system, whose origins go back to the earliest days of horse traction. The Sheffield Tramways Company served the city from 1873 to 1896, building up gradually to a maximum of 53 cars on 9¼ miles of route, which radiated to Tinsley, Brightside, Hillsborough, Nether Edge and Heeley. After 1896 the Corporation bought a further 24 horse cars and opened new horse routes to Walkley, Hunters Bar and Abbeydale. All these were replaced by electric tramways in 1899 to 1902, and new lines were opened to serve those parts of the city which were too hilly for the horse cars. The steepest electric routes were originally worked by single-deck cars, but permission was later granted to use double-deckers.

Routes extended in most directions from the city centre, and in two cases (Woodseats and Beauchief in 1927, and Darnall and Intake a year later), adjacent lines were converted into circular routes by sleeper-track connecting links. Another extension, to the Firth Park line in 1934, brought the tracks on to the main Barnsley road at Sheffield Lane Top, within eight miles of Barnsley's Worsborough Bridge. Three very short sections of route were abandoned in 1925-36, but these were all in narrow streets hardly suitable for trams, and the experiment proved to Sheffield Corporation that trams were better for city service, after which the policy was one of retention, modernisation and development of the tramways.

In contrast with other towns whose trams, often much rebuilt, would be made to last for 30 to 40 years, Sheffield Corporation adopted a praiseworthy policy of replacement by new vehicles after a 25-year life. The Corporation hardly ever stopped acquiring new trams during its first half-century of operation, and by 1940 only eleven of its 444 trams were more than about 26 years old, and more than half of them were less than ten. Thirty-five magnificent new cars were built as recently as 1950-52, bringing the total number of electric passenger trams to have operated in Sheffield to 884. Sheffield's final tramcar livery was cream all over, with three thin bands of blue, giving a refreshingly bright and cheerful appearance in strong contrast to the dark greens, dark reds and dark browns used by most other tramway fleets. Although some of the routes were five miles long, the maximum fare from 1931 to 1941 was only $1\frac{1}{2}$d. from the city to any suburban terminus, and $\frac{1}{2}$d. for children, with a 2d. cross-city stage. For ten years Sheffield tram passengers had paid an average fare of only 0.40 pence per mile, value for money which was not equalled in any "all-bus" community.

With its smooth tracks, excellent tramway paving, and comfortable and capacious four-wheel double-deck cars, the Sheffield system had a certain ultra-neat, tidy and highly-polished efficiency which placed it at once among the world's premier tramways. Sheffield was not blind to the uses of the motor bus, for it had a large fleet of them and did much early pioneer work on routes for which they are suitable, as well as having the first oil-engined bus in Britain. Sheffield's municipal bus fleet has always worked further out

Hidden away in an abandoned railway goods shed at Cullingworth, Yorkshire, for seven years to 1970, was Sheffield tram 513, one of the 35 post-war cars. This tram is now preserved by the North East Open Air Museum at Beamish.
(J. H. Price

into the country than most others, and the heavy trunk city services were operated exclusively by tramcars until disproportionate rises in the cost of new trams and track caused the Corporation to adopt a policy of replacement by motor buses in 1951. Two short sections were closed down at the beginning of 1952, followed by the other fifteen routes in 1954-60. The tramway may yet return to Sheffield (and Rotherham) in a more modern form, for a new tramway system is among the transport options being studied by the South Yorkshire Metropolitan County Council.

The two-mile gap from Conisbrough to a Doncaster outpost (at Warmsworth) has already been mentioned, and even disregarding the semi-tramway character of the early Mexborough trolleybus route the gap from the Old Toll Bar to Warmsworth is less than four miles as the crow flies. In addition to the route through Balby to Warmsworth other standard-gauge Doncaster Corporation tramways ran west to Hexthorpe, south to Oxford Street and to Hyde Park, east to the Racecourse, to Avenue Road and to Beckett Road, and north through Bentley to New Village. There was also a 1916-built route running several miles along the Great North Road to serve Britain's biggest colliery, at a point between Brodsworth and Adwick-le-Street, and this was almost entirely on a reserved sleeper track. The Bentley route originally had its own separate depot in Marshgate, as the Great Northern Railway refused to allow trams across its main line on the level, until the North Bridge was completed in 1911. From St. Leger Day in 1902 the undertaking handled enormous crowds to and from the racecourse, possibly the biggest race crowds ever experienced in Britain. The original 1902 fleet of 25 four-wheel open-top cars gradually increased to 47 by 1920 by the addition of 21 covered-top four-wheelers and one little demi-car. The Doncaster tramways were abandoned in 1928-35, mostly in favour of trolleybuses, which continued until 1963.

Doncaster made a definite break in the previous chain of tramways, for the next tramway town to the east was Hull. This physical separation, however, was combined with closeness in matters of practice, for these two towns used an unusual type of rail section, known as the centre-grooved rail. Although Hull and Doncaster were the only British examples in the electric era, the Liverpool horse tramways and the Dudley—Wolverhampton steam tramway had used the same type of rail in the 'eighties and 'nineties. In place of the orthodox rail surface with a space for the wheel flange on the inner side, there were two equal rail treads side by side, with the flange-way in the centre. The car wheels were shaped to correspond, with flanges projecting from the centre of the tyres. There were thus two bearing surfaces to each wheel, making for smoother running through points and other special work, in which connection the rail lengths were cut obliquely at the joints. A section can be seen today in the Hull transport museum, which also contains a Ryde Pier horse tram and a Portstewart steam tram engine.

Between Doncaster and Hull we cross at right-angles the 1882 authorised but unbuilt route of the Isle of Axholme and Marshland Tramways. This was to have been a 3ft. 6in. gauge steam tramway running the 14¼ miles from Haxey through Epworth and Crowle to Eastoft. The 4ft. 8½in. gauge

Axholme Joint Railway (L. & Y. and N.E.R.) was later built along a somewhat similar route, and this passes within three miles of the new trolleybus museum at Sandtoft, which, like the tramway museum at Crich, has been created and developed entirely by amateur enthusiasts.

Hull Corporation's 4ft. 8½in. gauge lines followed the five main roads out of town; two to the west, two to the east, and one to the north. To the north-west there was a rectangle of local routes extending along the Cotting-

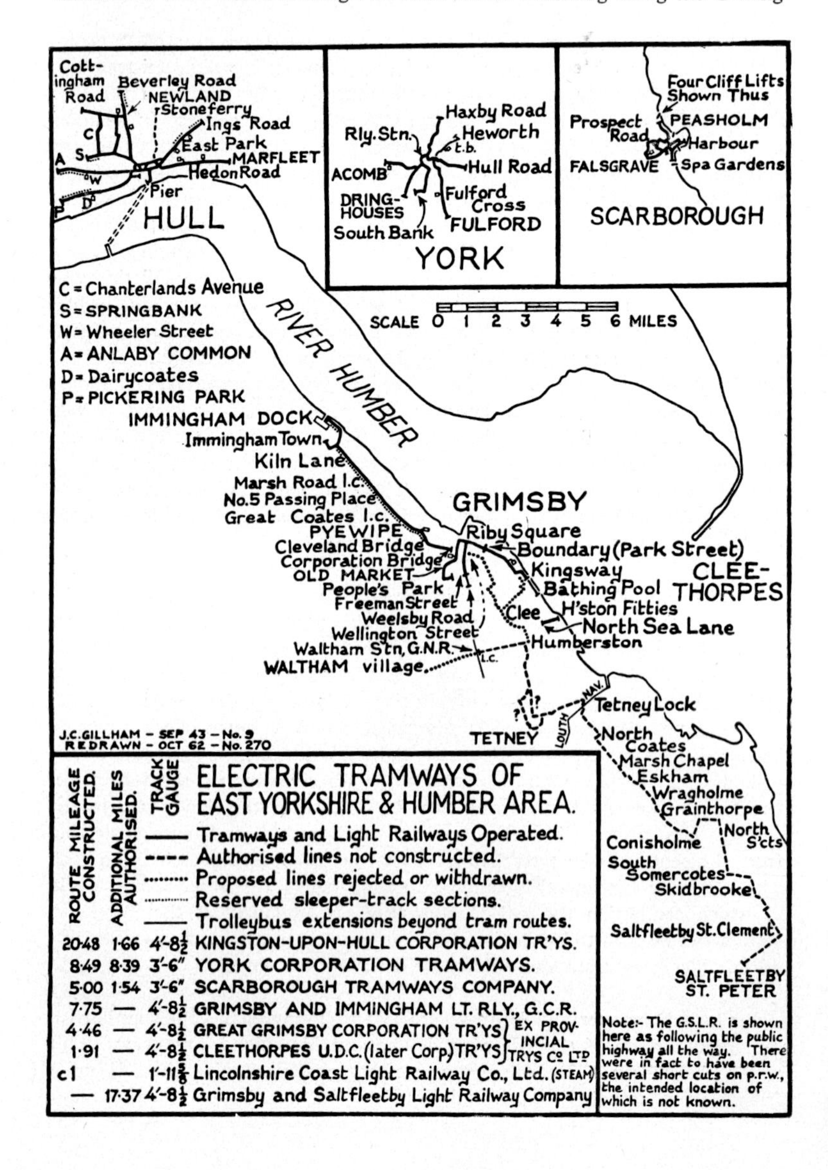

ham Road, whilst a short route ran through the narrow streets of the Old Town to the Corporation Pier. Most of these roads had previously been served by the horse trams of the Hull Street Tramways Co. Ltd., but Hedon Road had been served by steam trams of the Drypool and Marfleet Steam Tramways Co. Ltd. In the tramway era, traffic in Hull suffered greatly from the numerous railway level crossings, of which there were seven on tram routes, so catch points and semaphore signals were used here to protect the tramways, and interlocked with the railway equipment. In 1925 the Corporation, the L.N.E.R. and the Ministry of Transport agreed to a £1¼ million scheme to eliminate these seven crossings, and two others, and they agreed what proportions each authority should pay; but no more was done until 40 years later, when certain railways were closed and others diverted, and one crossing was replaced by a new road viaduct.

Hull had 21 miles of electric tramway, of which only a few yards was single track. The outer sections of the Holderness Road, Beverley Road, Spring Bank West, Anlaby Road and Hessle Road routes were all on reserved sleeper track, the two latter going well out from the city centre and reaching Anlaby Common and Pickering Park respectively. It was the intention to extend the Hessle Road tramway through to Hessle Village, and a route northwards to Stoneferry was partly constructed but never completed or opened. A notable achievement was the opening of a new bascule bridge (the North Bridge) across the River Hull in 1931, and the diversion thereto of the most heavily trafficked tramway artery. Hull had a large fleet of 179 electric cars, almost all of which were four-wheel totally-enclosed double-deckers with a characteristic domed roof, but owing to the very frequent stops and modest horsepower the operating speeds were relatively low. There was also one large bogie car, later sold to Erith.

Under a co-ordination scheme effected in 1934 with East Yorkshire Motor Services Ltd., all outer municipal routes went to the company, and so the Anlaby Road and Hessle Road tramways had to be pruned back at Wheeler Street and Dairycoates to the boundary of the new inner area, which was a pity, as the best sections of tramway were thus lost. In 1929 a proposal to introduce trolleybuses on the Preston Road motorbus route was defeated by

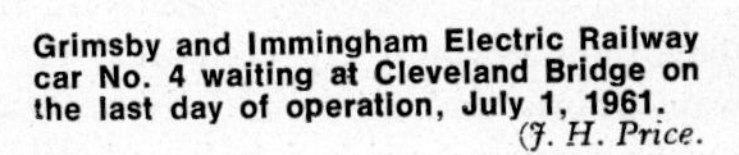

Grimsby and Immingham Electric Railway car No. 4 waiting at Cleveland Bridge on the last day of operation, July 1, 1961.
(J. H. Price.

the ratepayers, and the vehicles on order had to be altered to petrol buses. The short line to the Pier was replaced by motor buses in 1931 and the Hedon Road line in 1932; all other Hull tram routes were replaced by municipal trolleybuses during 1937-45, but the last trolleybus ran in 1964.

Obliquely across the Humber lies Immingham, with its large dock, formerly railway-owned and not too readily accessible by road. A useful purpose was thus served by a railway-owned electric light railway which the Great Central provided from Immingham Dock to Grimsby in 1912, replacing a short-lived steam railcar service on the adjacent railway line. In the opposite direction from the docks, a line north-westwards to Barton-upon-Humber was authorised in 1908 to the Barton and Immingham Light Railway Company, who intended to use electric traction, but this was taken over in 1912 by the Great Central Railway and in due course built as an ordinary steam line. The Grimsby line, starting inside the dock estate, emerged as a double-track tramway alongside a road, but at Immingham Town, where there was a short stretch of ordinary street tramway, the cars reversed, and then forsaking the road they took a direct south-eastward route to Grimsby parallel to the Humber bank, on a single track alongside a steam goods railway of the same ownership, and laid mainly in bull-head rail. A steady speed was maintained throughout this section, for there was a straight run of nearly five miles with only four intermediate request stops.

At the curiously named Pyewipe car sheds the electric track swerved away from the steam and, passing Cleveland Bridge Halt, abruptly became an ordinary street tramway, stopping frequently along Gilbey Road and Corporation Road until it terminated by the waiting room and parcels office at Corporation Bridge. The G.C.R. had powers to extend the Immingham line over Corporation Bridge when the Bridge was rebuilt, and to work through services into the town centre, but the bridge was not in fact rebuilt until 1928 and this proved to be too late.

The cars which provided the basic service to Immingham Dock were 12 very long bogie single-deckers, and normally a half-hour service was run, provided by two cars working day and night, which met at the fare stage known only as "No. 5 Passing Place". After the route was shortened in 1956, the basic two cars met at No. 8 Passing Place. Conveys of additional cars were run at shift times for dock and factory workers. Four shorter cars were bought for the intended through service into Grimsby, but saw little use. Had they survived until the post 1945 era they would have been very useful, for factory development along the Humber Bank made it necessary to buy three bogie single-deck cars from Newcastle-upon-Tyne Corporation in 1948, and a further 14 from the Gateshead and District Tramways Company in 1951. These cars were repainted in the bright green livery then used elsewhere for multiple-unit electric railway trains, and the same livery was applied to the ex-G.C.R. cars, replacing the former varnished teak or brown. The Grimsby terminus was cut back in 1956 from Corporation Bridge to Cleveland Bridge, but the rest of the line ran until the summer of 1961, needing as many as nineteen cars for the rush-hour schedule. As there is no road adjacent to the main part of the route the replacing buses have to take a very crooked course with a wide detour a long way inland, totalling twelve miles instead of the seven of the tramway, and journey time is nearly twice as much.

At Grimsby, a walk of a few yards over the Corporation Bridge brings us to Victoria Street, which carried the standard-gauge tramway from People's Park past the Old Market and Riby Square, over the Cleethorpes boundary at Park Street, and onwards to Cleethorpes (Kingsway). Most of this was originally a horse tramway, opened in 1881 by the Great Grimsby Street Tramways Company, who electrified the lines in 1901, with some minor extensions. A branch from Riby Square along Freeman Street was also electrified in 1901, although the proposed layout was not completed as the Great Northern Railway would not allow trams over their level crossing in Welholme Road to rejoin the main route at its People's Park terminus. A reserved-track extension along the Kingsway at Cleethorpes was authorised, but, because of a disagreement about the fares to be charged, only the first few yards were built. Six trailer cars were operated until 1918, mainly at football times, in addition to 31 four-wheel double-deck electric cars, and an open touring car was built in 1922, similar in appearance to the motor chara-bancs which the Provincial Company operated from Cleethorpes sea front.

The Great Grimsby Street Tramways Company, which operated both in Grimsby and in Cleethorpes, ran the entire system until 1925, when after a long-drawn-out legal process Grimsby Corporation acquired the lines in

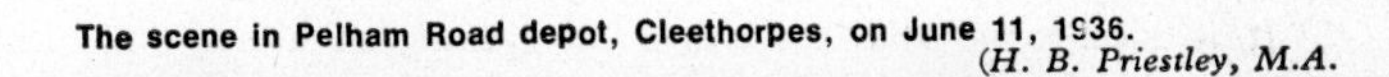

The scene in Pelham Road depot, Cleethorpes, on June 11, 1936.
(H. B. Priestley, M.A.

its own area. The twenty-two cars taken over were mostly worn out, so sixteen second-hand units were purchased from the Sunderland District Electric Tramways Ltd., and in 1926 the Freeman Street branch was replaced by trolleybuses and extended to Weelsby Road. The People's Park portion of the line closed in 1928, but the route from Old Market towards Cleethorpes continued to handle a very heavy traffic until replaced as far as Park Street by trolleybuses in November 1936. Some trams continued to run between Riby Square and Park Street until March 1937, continuing to Cleethorpes.

From 1925, the Great Grimsby Street Tramways Company (always a subsidiary of the Provincial Tramways Co. Ltd.) continued to work the line through Cleethorpes from Park Street to Kingsway, on which through joint services were continued after the Grimsby half was municipalised. Then in July, 1936, the Cleethorpes Urban District Council commenced its very brief career as a tramway operator by purchasing this route, which it converted to trolleybus operation exactly twelve months later, and extended to the Bathing Pool, resuming the through joint service to Grimsby which had been broken when the Grimsby tramway was abandoned. But as Cleethorpes had obtained a Charter of Incorporation in the intervening November, there were two separate régimes even during this short period, and successive ticket issues bore the headings "Cleethorpes U.D.C. Tramways Dept." and "Cleethorpes Corporation Tramways Dept.". The trolleybuses were transferred to a Grimsby-Cleethorpes Transport Joint Committee in 1957, and were replaced by motor buses in 1960.

It is nice to be able to record the opening of a new line, instead of another abandonment. At Humberston, near Cleethorpes, the new Lincolnshire Coast Light Railway Co. Ltd. opened its line to traffic in August 1960, running from North Sea Lane to a holiday camp near the Beach. It is a summer-only operation, on 1ft. 11⅝in. gauge track, with one steam and two diesel locomotives and four bogie passenger coaches.

Humberston might have had a narrow-gauge line sixty years earlier if the proposed Grimsby and Saltfleetby Light Railway had been built. This was to have run from Wellington Street, Grimsby, via Tetney Lock and North Somercotes to Saltfleetby, with branches from Humberston to Cleethorpes and to Waltham Station. The application of 1897 for a 3ft. gauge steam line was rejected, but it was renewed in 1898 with standard gauge and without the Grimsby to Humberston section. An Order was granted for this, but the promoters could not raise enough capital, especially for the expensive swing bridge over the Louth Navigation at Tetney Lock.

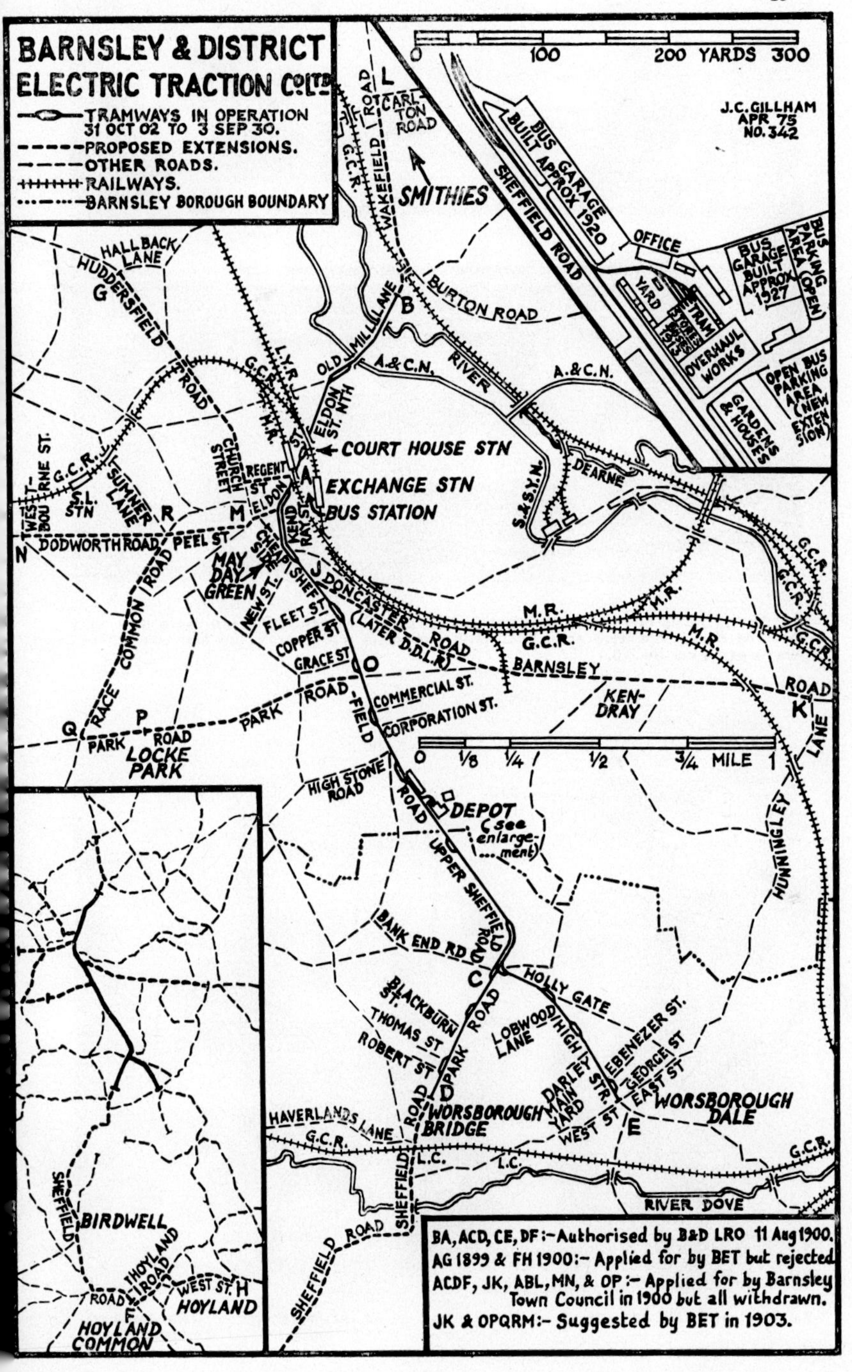
BARNSLEY & DISTRICT
ELECTRIC TRACTION Co. Ltd.
TRAMWAYS IN OPERATION 31 OCT 02 TO 3 SEP 30.
PROPOSED EXTENSIONS.
OTHER ROADS.
RAILWAYS.
BARNSLEY BOROUGH BOUNDARY
0 100 200 YARDS 300
J.C. GILLHAM
APR 75
NO. 342
BUS GARAGE BUILT APPROX 1920
SHEFFIELD ROAD
OFFICE
BUS GARAGE BUILT APPROX 1927
BUS PARKING AREA (OPEN)
YARD
TRAM
OVERHAUL WORKS
OPEN BUS PARKING AREA (NEW EXTENSION)
GARDENS & HOUSES
SMITHIES
CARLTON ROAD
WAKEFIELD ROAD
G.C.R.
BURTON ROAD
HALL BACK LANE
HUDDERSFIELD ROAD
OLD MILL LANE
ELDON ST. NTH
A. & C.N.
RIVER
DEARNE
COURT HOUSE STN
EXCHANGE STN
BUS STATION
S. & S.Y.N.
CHURCH STREET
REGENT ST
ELDON
KENDRAY ST.
CHEAPSIDE
G.C.R.
SUMNER LANE
S.L. STN
WESTBOURNE ST.
DODWORTH ROAD
PEEL ST
MAY DAY GREEN
NEW ST.
SHEFF
DONCASTER ROAD (LATER D.D.L.R.)
FLEET ST
COPPER ST
GRACE ST
M.R.
BARNSLEY ROAD
KENDRAY
RACE COMMON ROAD
PARK ROAD
LOCKE PARK
SHEFFIELD ROAD
COMMERCIAL ST.
CORPORATION ST.
0 1/8 1/4 1/2 3/4 MILE 1
HIGH STONE ROAD
DEPOT (see enlargement)
UPPER SHEFFIELD ROAD
HUNNINGLEY LANE
BANK END RD
HOLLY GATE
BLACKBURN ST.
THOMAS ST
ROBERT ST
PARK ROAD
LOBWOOD LANE
HIGH STR.
EBENEZER ST.
GEORGE ST
EAST ST
DARLEY MAIN YARD
WEST ST
WORSBOROUGH DALE
WORSBOROUGH BRIDGE
HAVERLANDS LANE
L.C.
RIVER DOVE
SHEFFIELD ROAD
BIRDWELL
HOYLAND ROAD
WEST ST.
HOYLAND
HOYLAND COMMON
A B C D E F G H J K L M N O P Q R
BA, ACD, CE, DF :- Authorised by B&D LRO 11 Aug 1900.
AG 1899 & FH 1900 :- Applied for by BET but rejected.
ACDF, JK, ABL, MN, & OP :- Applied for by Barnsley Town Council in 1900 but all withdrawn.
JK & OPQRM :- Suggested by BET in 1903.

The first 12 trams of the Barnsley and District Electric Traction Co. Ltd. were built with open top decks, but were soon fitted with removable top covers. The first one (shown here) was on car No. 10.

(courtesy The Yorkshire Traction Co. Ltd.

Barnsley tram No. 6 with a six-window top cover at Worsborough Dale terminus.

(R. B. Parr and T.M.S., block courtesy Tramway Review

An additional tram, No. 14, was built for Barnsley by Brush at Loughborough in 1912.
(Brush Electrical Engineering Co. Ltd., block courtesy Tramway Review

The original Barnsley trams were rebuilt with fixed top covers similar to that of No. 14, and ran in this form until the Barnsley tramways closed in Sepember 1930. This view shows car 3 at Smithies terminus in 1928.
(Science Museum, London, Whitcombe Collection

A E SMITH

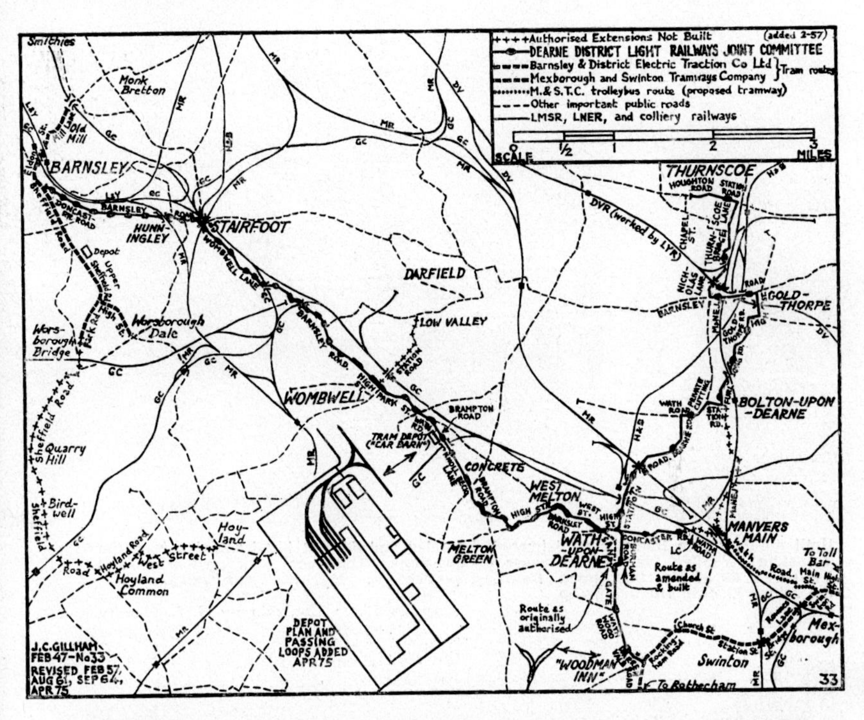

The Dearne District Light Railways, showing the routes traversed and the location of the passing loops.

On the opposite page are four views on the Dearne District Light Railways, taken at Wath-upon-Dearne (top left), Bolton Cutting (top right), near West Melton (lower left) and at Thurnscoe terminus (lower right). Single-deck cars were necessary because of a low brick arch at Wath station on the ex-Midland main line.

(S. L. Smith and T.M.S., block courtesy Tramway Review

Dearne District Light Railways No. 9 at Thurnscoe terminus in 1928. Most DDLR conductors were women.

(Science Museum Whitcombe Collection.

Until all their own trams were delivered, Barnsley and District hired vehicles from the Yorkshire (Woollen District) Tramways of Dewsbury. This local view postcard shows YWD tram 29 at May Day Green, Barnsley, probably in 1904. Both companies were in the British Electric Traction group.

(Barnsley Photo. Co., courtesy G. L. Gundry

At the Alhambra in Barnsley the Dearne District Light Railway's tracks met those of the Barnsley tramways, but were not connected. The conductress is turning the trolley of DDLR 22 for the 90-minute journey to Thurnscoe.

(Commercial postcard, courtesy C. C. Hall and Tramway Review

Nine Dearne District cars were sold after the system closed in 1933, five to Falkirk and four to Lytham St. Annes; Lytham 52 is seen here at Gynn Square, Blackpool, in 1934. The lower view shows Dearne District 14 at the depot, offered for sale after the system closed.

(Upper photograph Science Museum, London (Whitcombe Collection); lower photograph C. C. Hall

The first sixteen cars of the Mexborough and Swinton Tramways Company ran on the Dolter surface contact system. The Dolter studs are visible between the rails in this view of Bridge Street, Swinton. This system of current collection proved unsuccessful and was replaced by overhead wires in August, 1908.

(courtesy C. C. Hall and Tramway Review

Mexborough and Swinton No. 18 at the top of Rawmarsh Hill. Because of a low bridge, the cars were fitted with special turtle-back top covers and the trolley base was fitted on the side of the roof.

(Commercial postcard (ELS Series), courtesy C. C. Hall and Tramway Review

Mexborough and Swinton Tramways in the 1920s. Above, No. 18 in Station Road, Swinton, in 1922; below, No. 11 in 1928, a year before the trams were replaced by single-deck trolleybuses.

(No. 18, ELS Series Commercial postcard; No. 11, Whitcombe Collection, Science Museum

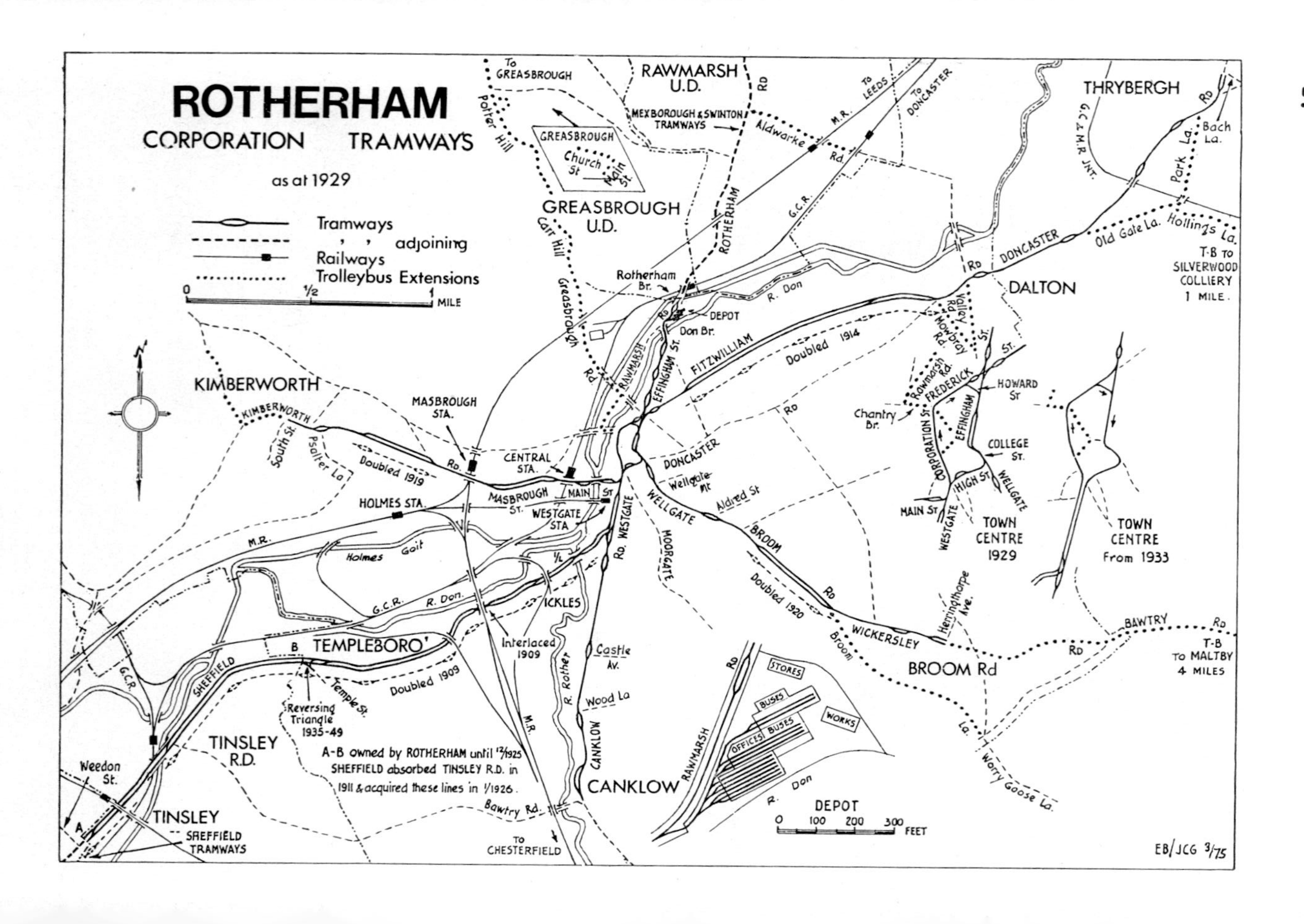

ROTHERHAM
CORPORATION TRAMWAYS
as at 1929
Tramways
" " adjoining
Railways
Trolleybus Extensions
0 1/2 1 MILE
To GREASBROUGH
RAWMARSH U.D.
MEXBOROUGH & SWINTON TRAMWAYS
Aldwarke Rd.
M.R.
To LEEDS
To DONCASTER
THRYBERGH
G.C. & M.R. JNT.
Bach La.
Park La.
Hollings La.
Old Gate La.
T-B to SILVERWOOD COLLIERY 1 MILE.
DALTON
DONCASTER Rd
GREASBROUGH
Church St
Main St
Potter Hill
GREASBROUGH U.D.
Carr Hill
Greasbrough Rd.
ROTHERHAM
G.C.R.
Rotherham Br.
R. Don
DEPOT
Don Br.
RAWMARSH Rd
EFFINGHAM St.
FITZWILLIAM
Doubled 1914
Valley Rd
Mowbray Rd.
Rawmarsh Rd.
FREDERICK St.
HOWARD St
EFFINGHAM
Chantry Br.
CORPORATION St
COLLEGE St.
HIGH St
WELLGATE
MAIN St
WESTGATE
TOWN CENTRE 1929
TOWN CENTRE From 1933
KIMBERWORTH
South St.
Psalter La
Doubled 1919
MASBROUGH STA.
Rd.
CENTRAL STA.
MASBROUGH St.
MAIN St
WESTGATE STA
HOLMES STA.
DONCASTER Rd
Wellgate Mt
Aldred St
WELLGATE
BROOM Rd
Doubled 1920
WICKERSLEY
Herringthorpe Ave.
BAWTRY Rd
T-B To MALTBY 4 MILES
BROOM Rd
Broom La.
Worry Goose La.
MOORGATE
Rd. WESTGATE
M.R.
Holmes Goit
G.C.R.
R. Don.
ICKLES
Interlaced 1909
TEMPLEBORO'
SHEFFIELD
Doubled 1909
Temple St.
Reversing Triangle 1935-49
R. Rother
Castle Av.
Wood La
CANKLOW
CANKLOW
A-B owned by ROTHERHAM until 12/1925
SHEFFIELD absorbed TINSLEY R.D. in 1911 & acquired these lines in 1/1926.
TINSLEY R.D.
Weedon St.
TINSLEY
SHEFFIELD TRAMWAYS
Bawtry Rd.
To CHESTERFIELD
RAWMARSH Rd
STORES
BUSES
WORKS
OFFICES
R. Don
DEPOT
0 100 200 300 FEET
EB/JCG 3/75

Rotherham Corporation commenced tramway operation with 27 open-top and three single-deck cars. This view is of car 26, built at Preston in 1903.

(*T.M.S.*

One of Rotherham's original cars, reposted with six saloon windows and fitted with a domed-roof top cover, on the Sheffield—Rotherham through service in 1933.

(*M. J. O'Connor*

Three operators' services met in the centre of Rotherham. The scene above, photographed by M. J. O'Connor in 1933, shows a Rotherham tram on the Canklow service in Frederick Street, with a Mexborough and Swinton trolleybus and a Sheffield tram in the background. The lower picture shows College Square, Rotherham in 1908, with Sheffield car 82, Rotherham 12, and Rotherham and Mexborough open-top cars.

(M. J. O'Connor/E.L.S. Series, blocks courtesy Tramway Review

Rotherham 3, one of four replacement cars bought from English Electric in 1920, at Exchange Street terminus, Sheffield, in 1933.

(M. J. O'Connor

In 1934/35 Rotherham Corporation bought eleven single-ended cars for use on the through service to Sheffield which had loops at each terminus. They were virtually a trolleybus body mounted on a tramcar truck.

(W. J. Haynes

During the 1939-45 war, Rotherham Corporation required two additional trams for steelworkers traffic to Ickles and Templeborough. Car No. 12 (above) was converted from an earlier Rotherham tram kept as a works car, and car No. 14 (below) was obtained from Leeds Corporation.

(C. C. Hall and Tramway Review

The Sheffield—Rotherham joint tram service in August, 1948. The upper view shows Sheffield 146 and Rotherham 11 at College Square terminus in Rotherham; the lower view shows Rotherham 9 and 11 at Exchange Street terminus in Sheffield, with Sheffield 255 in the background.

(*W. A. Camwell*

Rotherham Corporation No. 16, rebuilt in 1923 from an ex-Oldham bogie single-decker for use on the Broom Road service.

(Science Museum, London, Whitcombe Collection

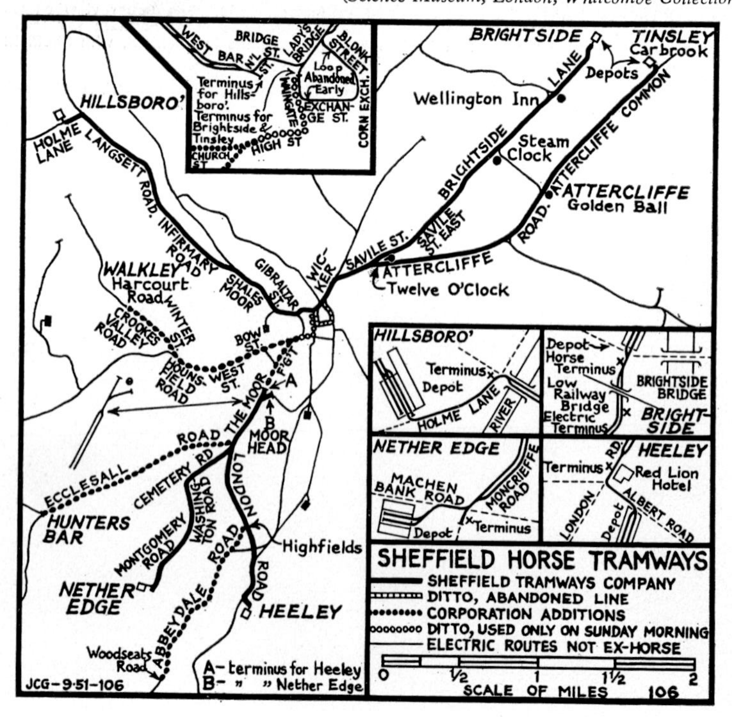

Sheffield Tramways Company Eades Reversible horse tram of 1886 at Nether Edge depot. Horse trams ran in Sheffield from 1873 to 1902; the Corporation took over from the Company in 1896.
(Tramway Review

Sheffield's first electric trams waiting in Tinsley depot prior to the inauguration of electric service on September 5, 1899.

Many of Sheffield's first electric cars were single-deck because of steep hills, but some of the single-deckers were rebuilt with top decks, and others were sold or converted to snowploughs. No. 208, seen here in 1906, was the first to be rebuilt as a double-decker.
(Sheffield Transport Department

Sheffield's open-top tramcars were soon fitted with short top covers of the type shown on car 13. The scene is Fitzalan Square in 1913, and also shows single-deck car 192 on the Firth Park route.

(T.M.S.

Sheffield Corporation established a fine tradition of decorated and illuminated tramcars to mark special events. This example ran during the visit of H.M. The King and Queen on July 12, 1905.

(Furniss, courtesy G. L. Gundry

Sheffield Corporation No. 56, one of six single-deck cars built at Preston in 1899. This car was later sold to the Glossop tramways.

(*Tramway and Railway World*

Sheffield Corporation had 150 trams of this type, built between 1919 and 1927. The last three survivors 42, 52 and 497, were withdrawn after a farewell tour on April 28, 1957.

(*R. J. S. Wiseman, B.A.*

The last Sheffield trams to bear the traditional dark blue livery lined in gold were these straight-sided cars built from 1928 to 1935. Three of them are shown in the upper view of football cars in Wolseley Road, awaiting the end of a Sheffield United match. The lower view on the Abbey Lane reserved track shows similar car 98 repainted in the post-1936 cream livery.

(R. J. S. Wiseman, B.A.

Sixty-seven of these attractive domed-roof cars were built by the Sheffield Corporation at Queens Road works betwen 1936 and 1939.

(Sheffield Transport Department

A further 14 domed-roof cars were built between 1941 and 1944 to replace vehicles lost through war damage.

(R. Brook

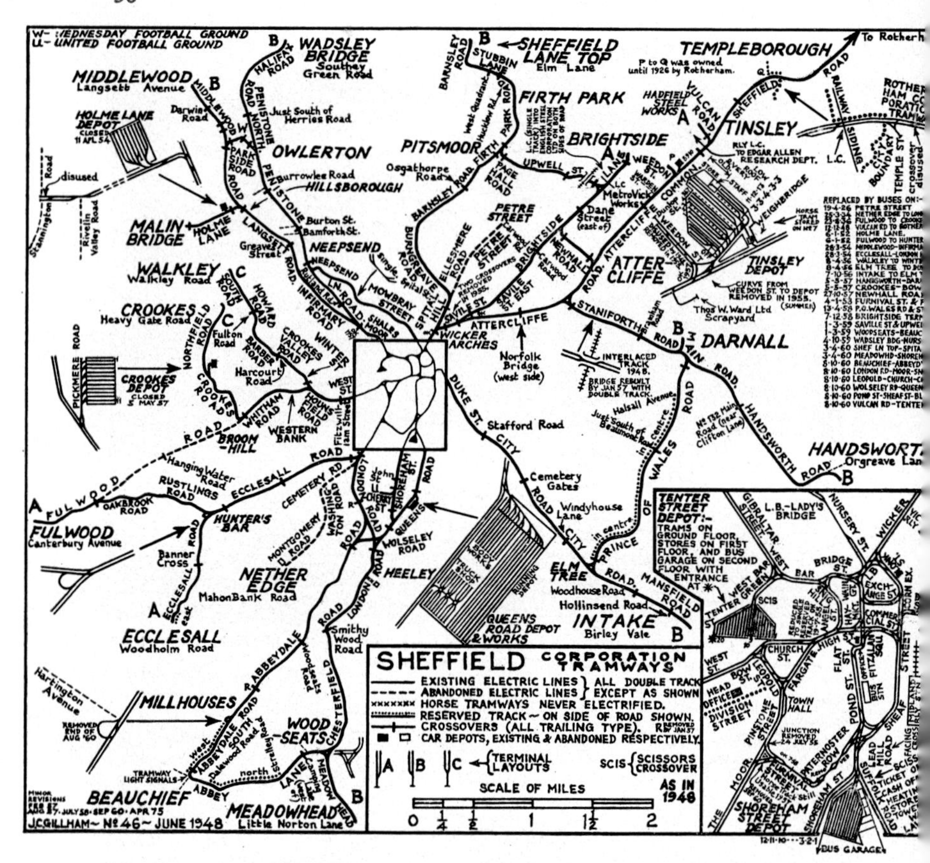

The Sheffield tramway system in 1948. Service numbers were not used on the trams.

Sheffield's method of relaying street track gave a smooth non-skid surface.
(D. D. Shaw

In 1941-42, Sheffield Corporation bought 14 cars from Newcastle and 10 from Bradford. They were rebuilt at Sheffield with enclosed top decks before re-entering service. The ex-Newcastle cars (above) ran in blue and cream, but the Bradford cars (below) ran in a wartime grey-green livery.

(Sheffield Transport Department

In 1946 Sheffield Corporation built prototype car 501, known as the Jubilee type because it marked 50 years of municipal operation. This was the first British tramcar to have fluorescent lighting.

(*Sheffield Transport Department*

Thirty-five cars similar to 501 were built for Sheffield in 1950-52 by Charles Roberts & Co. Ltd. No. 535 is shown here on the reserved track between Millhouses and Beauchief on January 19, 1955.

(*R. J. S. Wiseman, B.A.*

Right: **A scene on the last night of Sheffield's tramways, October 8, 1960. Sheffield 46, now preserved at Crich was one of the trams in the final procession.**
(M. A. Ward

Below: **Sheffield stores car 349 was used as a decorated and illuminated tramcar during Last Tram Week in October, 1960.**
(T. W. Ward Ltd. block courtesy T.M.S

Electric Tramcar Fleets — South Yorkshire and Humberside

All cars were four-wheel double-deck unless otherwise stated.
Seating figures shown thus : 22/34 are for lower and upper decks respectively.

Barnsley and District Electric Traction Company

4ft. 8½in. gauge, opened 31 October 1902, closed 3 September 1930.

Car Numbers	Type (as built)	Year built	Builder	Seats	Truck	Motors	Controllers
1—10	Open top	1902	Brush	22/26	Brush Type A	Brush 1000B 2 x 30hp	Brush
11—12	Open top	1903	Brush	22/26	Brush Type A	Brush 1000B 2 x 30hp	Brush
13	Demi car	Bought 1905	BEC	20	BEC Special	Brush	Raworth
14	Balcony	1912	Brush	?	Brill 21E	?	?
—	Water car	1903	Brush	—	Brush Type A	Brush 1000B 2 x 30hp	Brush

Cars 1—12 were fitted with short top covers by Milnes Voss and Brush in 1903-4; these were rebuilt with extended canopy roofs in 1912-14. Car 13 was built in 1904 for the Yorkshire Woollen District Tramways as No. 59. YWD cars 19, 20 and 29 ran in Barnsley during 1903-4.

Dearne District Light Railways

4ft. 8½in. gauge, opened 14 July 1924, closed 30 September 1933.

Car Numbers	Type (as built)	Year built	Builder	Seats	Truck	Motors	Controllers
1—25	Single deck	1923-24	EE	36	Peckham P22	DK 30B 2 x 40hp	DK DB1 Form K3
26—30	Single deck	1924	EE	36	Peckham P22	DK 30B 2 x 40hp	DK DB1 Form K3

Four cars were reseated about 1927 with two-and-one transverse to seat 31. These four and one other were sold after closure to Falkirk, becoming Falkirk 11, 12, 17, 18 and 19. Four were sold to Lytham St. Annes as Lytham 51—54; the trucks and equipments of the other 21 cars were sold to Hull.

Doncaster Corporation Tramways

Centre groove rail, 4ft. 8½in. gauge (4ft. 7⅝in. between groove centres), opened 2 June 1902, closed 8 June 1935.

Car Numbers	Type (as built)	Year built	Builder	Seats	Truck	Motors	Controllers
1—15	Open top	1902	ER&TCW	22/34	Brill 21E	DK 25A 2 x 25hp	DK DB1 Form B
16—20	Open top	1903	ER&TCW	22/34	Brill 21E	DK 25A 2 x 25hp	DK DB1 Form B
21—25	Open top	1903	ER&TCW	22/34	Brill 21E	DK 25A 2 x 25hp	DK DB1 Form B
26—31	Balcony	1913	UEC	58	Peckham P22	DK 20 2 x 40hp	DK DB1 Form K3
32	Balcony	1913	UEC	32/42	Peckham radial	DK 20 2 x 40hp	DK DB1 Form K3
33—36	Balcony	1916	UEC	26/40	Peckham P22	DK 20 2 x 40hp	DK DB1 Form K3
37	Demi car	Bought 1916	Milnes Voss	20	M&G 40	Westinghouse 2 x 27hp	Raworth
38—47	Balcony	1920	EE	26/40	Peckham P22 (EE)	DK 30B 2 x 40hp	DK DB1 Form K3
—	Water car	1902	ER&TCW	—	Brill 21E	DB 25A 2 x 25hp	DK DB1 Form B

Sixteen top covers were obtained from UEC and Brush (four UEC in 1909, twelve in 1913) and were fitted to cars 5—16 and 22—25. Car 37 was built in 1906 for Erith UDC. The Brill 21E trucks were later fitted with wide wing axleboxes, except for those of 7 and 14 (altered to P22) and 23 and 24 (replaced by P22). The DB1 Form B controllers on cars 1—25 were later replaced by BTH B18 type. Open top car 21 served as decorated car and tower wagon. Car 32 later received a Peckham P22 truck. There was also a sand and salt trailer rebuilt from a York horse car. The trams were replaced by trolleybuses, which operated from 22 August 1928 to 14 December 1963.

Great Grimsby Street Tramways Company

4ft. 8½in. gauge, opened 7 December 1901, closed 17 July 1937.

Car Numbers	Type (as built)	Year built	Builder	Seats	Truck	Motors	Controllers
1—22	Open top	1900	ER&TCW	22/34	Brill 21E	Walker 33S 2 x 25hp	DK S7
23—24	Open top	1901	ER&TCW	22/34	Brill 21E	Walker 33S 2 x 25hp	DK S7
25, 26, 28	Open top	(1903-04)	Falkenried (rebuilt by GGST)	22/34	Falkenried	Steel Motor Co 2 x 25hp	Johnson USA
27	Enclosed top	(1903)	Falkenried rebuilt by GGST)	28/35	Falkenried	Steel Motor Co. 2 x 25hp	Johnson USA
29, 30	Open top	1903	ER&TCW	22/34	Brill 21E	Walker 33S 2 x 25hp	DK S7
31-34	Open top trailers	1899	ER&TCW	20/26	Trunnions	—	—
35, 36	Ex-horse trailers	—	?	?	Trunnions	—	—
37	Balcony	Bought 1906	ER&TCW	?	Brill 21E	DK 25A 2 x 25hp	DK DB1 Form B
38	Single deck	Bought 1915	ER&TCW	30	Brill 21E	DK 25A 2 x 25hp	DK DE1 Form A
31-34	Open top, ex trailer	(1920)	ER&TCW	20/33	Brill 21E	Walker 33S 2 x 25hp	DK S7
39	Open top	1925	GGST	?	MSCC 21E	?	DK DB1 Form D
40 (I)	Open single deck	1922	GGST	40	Brill 21E	?	?
35, 36 (II)	Balcony	1926	GGST	?	MSCC 21E	?	DK DB1 Form D
57-59	Balcony	1927	GGST	?	MSCC 21E	?	DK DB1 Form D
40 (II), 60	Balcony	1928	GGST	?	MSCC 21E	?	DK DB1 Form D
1-3 (II), 22-30 (II)	Open top	Bought 1929	Brush	55	Brill 21E	?	?

Notes

Car No. 3 (I) received an Angier Empire Equalizer truck in 1902 but later reverted to Brill 21E.

Cars 5—12 and 18—22 received open balcony top covers in 1908 (seating 22/38); cars 5, 6, 10 and 19 were retrucked and received DK 25A motors and DK DB1 Form C controllers at the same time.

Cars 23, 24, 29 received "White" enclosed top covers in 1904 but these were later altered to open balcony.

Cars 25—28 were built in 1898 as 50-seat single-deck combination cars by Waggonfabrik Falkenried, Hamburg, for the Alexandra Park Electric Railway in North London, and were resold to Grimsby (via Dick Kerr) in 1899 and rebuilt as double-deck cars by Grimsby in 1903-4. The original trucks and equipments were replaced in 1908 by the Brill 21E trucks, Walker 33S motors and S7 controllers from cars 5, 6, 10 and 19. Car 27 was further rebuilt shortly afterwards with balcony top and new lower saloon after collison damage; cars 26 and 28 were used as rail grinders.

Car 37 was built for exhibition purposes by ER&TCW in 1904 and sold to Grimsby in 1906.

Car 38 was built in 1900 as Southport Corporation 13.

Car 39 received a balcony top cover in 1926.

Car 40 (I) was sold to Portsdown & Horndean in 1925.

The two ex-horse trailers were sold to Lincoln in 1918 (Lincoln 32, 33).

Cars 4—21 and 31—34 were taken over by Grimsby Corporation in 1925.

Cars 1, 23, 24 and 29 were renumbered 11, 18, 12, and 8 respectively in 1929.

Cars 1—3 (II) and 22—30 (II) were built by Brush in 1905 for the Gosport and Fareham Tramways and initially ran at Grimsby as open-top cars, but Nos. 2, 3, 27 and 30 were given balcony top covers by 1933.

All surviving GGST cars were taken over by Cleethorpes Council on 15 July 1936 and withdrawn in 1937. These trams were replaced by trolleybuses, which ran from 18 July 1937 to 4 June 1960 (merged with Grimsby from 1 January 1957 as Grimsby-Cleethorpes Transport Joint Committee).

Grimsby Corporation Tramways

4ft. 8½in. gauge, commenced operation 6 April 1925, closed 31 March 1937.

Car Numbers	Type (as built)	Year built	Builder	Seats	Truck	Motors	Controllers
4—21, 31—34	These cars were taken over in 1925 from Great Grimsby Street Tramways Company; for details see preceding list. Most were withdrawn in 1926-28. Ten were balcony cars and the other twelve were open-top cars.						
41—56	Balcony	Bought 1925	Brush	22/29	Brush Aa	GE 67 2 x 40hp	BTH B18

Cars 41—56 were built in 1913 for Sunderland District Electric Tramways Ltd. (Nos. 16—30 and 33). Cars 43 and 47 were hired by Cleethorpes from 1 April to 18 July 1937.
The Grimsby Corporation Tramways were replaced by trolleybuses, which ran from 3 October 1926 to 4 June 1960 (merged with Cleethorpes from 1 January 1957 as Grimsby-Cleethorpes Transport Joint Committee).

Grimsby and Immingham Electric Railway

4ft. 8½in. gauge, opened 15 May 1912, closed 1 July 1961. All cars were eight-wheel bogie cars.

Car Numbers	Type (as built)	Year built	Builder	Seats	Trucks	Motors	Controllers
1—4	Single deck	1911	Brush	64(a)	Brush equal wheel	DK 9 2 x 50hp	DK DB1 Form K4
5—8	Single deck	1911	Brush	40(a)	as 1—4	DK 10B 2 x 35hp	DK DB1 Form K4
9—12	Single deck	1913	Brush	64(a)	as 1—4	DK 9 2 x 50hp	DK DB1 Form K4
13—16	Single deck	1915	Brush /GCR (Note b)	64(a)	as 1—4	DK 9 2 x 50hp	DK DB1 Form K4
6—8 (II)	Single deck	Bought 1948	Hurst Nelson	40	Peckham P25	CP C160 2 x 50hp	BTH B510A?
17—33	Single deck	Bought 1951	See note (c)	48	Brill 39E1	DK 31A 2 x 50hp	DK DB1 Form K3
DE320224	Works car	Bought 1951	G&DT	(48)	Brill 39E1	DK 31A 2 x 50hp	DK DB1 Form K3

Notes

(a) Plus four double folding seats in central luggage compartments.
(b) Ordered from Brush but believed to have been completed at Great Central Railway Carriage Works, Dukinfield.
(c) 17, 21, 23, 28, 29, 32, 33 built by Brush, others by Gateshead.
Car 5 was used as a works car until replaced by DE320224.
Cars 6—8 (II) were built in 1901 for Newcastle-upon-Tyne Corporation (Nos. 29, 42, 77) and rebuilt by Newcastle in 1932-33.
Cars 17—33 were built in 1921-28 for the Gatehead and District Tramways Company. Their Gateshead numbers were respectively 57, 18, 9, 5, 56, 7, 20, 3, 6, 10, 16, 58, 1, 8, 11, 60 and 59.
Works car DE320224 was built in 1925 as Gateshead 17.

Mexborough and Swinton Tramways Company

4ft. 8½in. gauge, opened 6 February 1907, closed 9 March 1929.

Car Numbers	Type (as built)	Year built	Builder	Seats	Truck	Motors	Controllers
1—16	Open top	1906	Brush	22/32	M&G Radial	GE 58 2 x 35hp	BTH B18
17—20	Balcony	1908	Brush	22/32	Brush 21E	GE 58 2 x 35hp	Westinghouse 90M
—	Water car	1908?	?	—	?	?	?

The Mexborough trams ran on the Dolter surface-contact system until 30 July 1908.
Twelve cars of series 1—16 received Brush top covers in 1908 and two more in 1912; the other two open top cars (10 and 14) were sold in 1911 to Dewsbury and Ossett. The remaining cars of the 1—16 series received Brush 21E trucks in 1919-23. Cars 7 and 15 were sold to Dewsbury and Ossett in 1929.
The trams were replaced in 1928-29 by trolleybuses, which operated until 26 March 1961.
Other trolleybuses had been running since 31 August 1915.

City of Hull Tramways

Centre groove rail, 4ft. 8½in. gauge (4ft. 7⅝in between groove centres), opened 5 July 1899, closed 30 June 1945.

Car Numbers	Type (as built)	Year built	Builder	Seats	Truck	Motors	Controllers
1—15	Open top	1898	Milnes	22/29	Brill 21E	Siemens	Siemens
16—25	Open top	1899	Milnes	22/29	Brill 21E	Westinghouse 2 x 25hp	Westinghouse 90 ?
26—30	Open top	1899	Brill	22/29	Brill 21E	Westinghouse 2 x 25hp	Westinghouse 90 ?
31—60	Open top	1900	Brush	22/29	Brill 21E	Westinghouse 2 x 25hp	Westinghouse 90 ?
61—65	Open top	1900	ER&TCW	22/31	Brill 21E	Westinghouse 2 x 25hp	Westinghouse 90 ?
66—90	Open top	1900 (a)	Milnes	22/29	Brill 21E	BTH 2 x 25hp	BTH B3 ?
91—100	Open top	1901	Hurst Nelson	22/31	Brill 21E	BTH 2 x 25hp	BTH B3 ?
101—105 (a)	Open top trailers	1898	Milnes	22/29	trunnions	—	—
106—125 (a)	Open top trailers	1899	Milnes	22/29	trunnions	—	—
101 (II) (d)	Open top bogie	1900	Milnes	30/39	Brill 22E bogies	Westinghouse (d)	Westinghouse
102—116 (II)	Balcony (b)	1903	Milnes	22/34	Brill 21E	Westinghouse 2 x 25hp	Westinghouse
117—122 (II)	Balcony	1909	UEC	22/34	M&G 21EM	DK 9A (c) 2 x 40hp	BTH B18
123—125 (II)	Balcony	1909	HCT	22/34	M&G 21EM	Siemens 2 x 38hp	Siemens Type S
126—136	Balcony	1910	HCT	22/34	M&G 21EM	Siemens 2 x 38hp	Siemens Type S
137—160	Balcony	1912	Brush	22/34	Brill 21E	Siemens 2 x 33hp	Siemens Type S
161—180	Balcony	1915	Brush	22/40	Brill 21E	Siemens 2 x 35hp	Siemens Type S
101 (III)	Enclosed	1923	EE	24/42	EE Rayner	DK 85A 2 x 42hp	DK DB1 Form K3
113 (II)	Enclosed	1925	HCT	22/40	Brill 21E	?	Westinghouse
1—2	Water car	1899	Brill	—	Brill 21E	Westinghouse 2 x 25hp	Westinghouse
—	Rail grinder	1916	HCT	—	Brill 21E	BTH ?	BTH ?

Notes

(a) Cars 101—125 (I) were built in 1898-99 as trailers; motorised and renumbered 66—90 in 1900-01.
(b) Cars 102—116 (II) were built by G. F. Milnes as open top cars but were fitted with Milnes Voss top covers before entering service.
(c) Siemens motors in car 119.
(d) Car 101 (II) was fitted with DK9A 40 h.p. motors in 1909 and was sold in 1916 to Erith. It ran until 1933 as Erith 19, later LPTB 19D.

Rebuilding of cars

Cars 1—60 and 66—90 were built without canopies; cars 1—15 were given new Siemens motors in 1918-19. Cars 61—65 and 91—100 were built with short canopies.
Cars 61—65, 67—72, 74—80, 83—100 received movable top covers in 1903-05.
Cars 1—116 received short fixed top covers between 1905 and 1909, with seating increased to 22/30.
Car 101 (II) received a short top cover about 1909, with seating increased to 30/40.
Cars 35, 36, 61—66, 70, 76, 82, 94, 100, 117—122 and 137—160 received covered balconies in 1915-20.
Cars 1—34, 36—59, 67—81, 83—93, 95—99, 102—116 and 123—136 were rebuilt all-enclosed between 1920 and 1931, with seating increased to 22/40.
Cars 63, 94, 100, 117—122, 138—140, 142, 144—156, 158—160, 163, 164, 169, 170 and 173—176 were rebuilt all-enclosed in 1933-35, using top covers from other cars then being withdrawn; seating 22/40.
Two Peckham P22A trucks were bought about 1927 and were fitted to cars 109 and 120.
About 65 cars received secondhand DK 30B 40 h.p. motors and DK K3B controllers in 1933-35, including 21 cars retrucked with Peckham P22 trucks from the Dearne District Light Railway, 15 cars retrucked with Brill 21E trucks from Rochdale, and other cars believed to have been retrucked with Peckham P22 trucks from Doncaster. Some GEC 40 h.p. motors were also purchased second-hand. 42 of the retrucked and remotored cars were sold to Leeds City Transport in 1942-45, becoming Leeds 446—487. 30 of the original 21E trucks were sold to Recife (Brazil) in 1934-35.
Car 96 became a single-deck stores car and snowplough in 1933 and was sold in 1945 to Leeds.
The trams were mostly replaced by trolleybuses, which operated from 25 July 1937 to 31 October 1964.

Rotherham Corporation Tramways

4ft. 8½in. gauge, opened 31 January 1903, closed 13 November 1949.

Car Numbers	Type (as built)	Year built	Builder	Seats	Truck	Motors	Controllers
1—12	Open top	1902	ER&TCW	22/34	Brill 21E	DK 25A 2 x 25hp	DK DE1 Form B
13—15	Single deck	1903	ER&TCW	28	Brill 21E	DK 25A 2 x 25hp	DK DE1 Form B
16—30	Open top	1903	ER&TCW	22/34	Brill 21E	DK 25A 2 x 25hp	DK DB1 Form C
31	Water car	1905	UEC	—	Brill 21E	DK 25A 2 x 25hp	DK DB1 Form F
32—34	Balcony	1909	UEC	72	Note (a)	DK 9A1 2 x 40hp	DK DB1 Form K1
35—37	Balcony	1909	UEC	22/34	Note (a)	DK 9A1 2 x 40hp	DK DB1 Form K1
38—49	Single deck bogie	Bought 1916	ER&TCW	38	Brill 27G	DK 25A 4 x 25hp	DK DB1 Form D
50—59	Enclosed top	Bought 1917	ER&TCW	22/34	Brill 21E	DK 25A 2 x 25hp	DK DB1 Form D
60—68 (?)	Balcony Note (b)	1920	EE	?	Brill 21E	Note (b)	Note (b)
1—4 (II)	Balcony	1920	EE	22/38?	Preston 21E	DK 30B 2 x 40hp	DK DB1 Form K3
1—6 (III)	Enclosed single ended	1934	EE	27/36	EMB Hornless	GEC 2 x 40hp	Note (c)
7—11 (III)	Enclosed single ended	1935	EE	27/36	EMB Hornless	GEC WT294 x 40hp?	GEC KN7
14 (II)	Enclosed	Note (d)	LCT	24/36	Brill 21E	DK 9A 2 x 40hp	DK DB1 Form K3

Notes

(a) Cars 32—37 were mounted on UEC Preston Compensating 4-wheel trucks.

(b) Cars 60—68 were new EE lower deck bodies bought in 1920 and fitted by Rotherham with trucks, equipments and top covers from cars in series 5—12 and 17—26. They were soon renumbered into these series, replacing cars withdrawn. The other 1902-3 cars were rebuilt by Rotherham in 1925-27, and both series received Craven trucks, GEC 40 h.p. motors and BTH controllers; some of these motors were re-used in single-ended cars 1—6 of 1934. Details of car renumbering in 1923-27 and 1934-35 are given in **Tramway Review 57**.

(c) GEC TE5 RIZ controllers at front end, DK DB1 K3 at rear end.

(d) Car 14 (II) was built in 1908 by Leeds City Tramways as Leeds 125 (125A from 1927) and was hired by Rotherham in 1942 and bought in 1948. The open-balcony top deck was enclosed by Rotherham.

Three Milnes Voss top covers were bought in 1905 and fitted to cars 28—30.

21 UEC domed-roof top covers were bought in 1906-13 and fitted to most cars in series 1—12 and 16—27. Single-deck cars 13-15 were rebuilt as open balcony domed-roof double deck cars in 1908.

Cars 38—49 were built in 1902 for Oldham Corporation. Eight were resold to Walthamstow Corporation in 1919. One was placed on a Cravens 4-wheel truck in 1921 and renumbered 28. Two more were rebuilt in 1923 as 4-wheel 30-seat cars on Cravens trucks with DK 30B 40 h.p. motors and DK Form L3 controllers, and renumbered 16 and 27.

Cars 50—59 were built in 1903 for the London County Council (class B). They were altered to open-balcony condition by Rotherham in 1922 and renumbered 39—48. Cars 40—47 were resold to Sheffield in 1926.

One original car fitted with domed-roof top cover was retained after 1935 and numbered 12, but was not the original car of this number. It was altered to all-enclosed form in 1942.

The Rotherham trams were mostly replaced by trolleybuses, which ran until 2 October 1965. Other trolleybuses had been running since 3 October 1912.

Sheffield Corporation Tramways

4ft. 8½ in. gauge, opened 5 September 1899, closed 8 October 1960.

Car Numbers	Type (as built)	Year built	Builder	Seats	Truck	Motors	Controllers
1—25	Open top	1899	Milnes	22/29	Peckham Cantilever	BTH GE52 2 x 25hp	BTH B13
26—38	Open top	1900	Milnes	22/29	Peckham Cantilever	BTH GE52 2 x 25hp	BTH B13
39—50	Single deck	1899	Milnes	28	Peckham Cantilever	BTH GE52 2 x 25hp	BTH B6
51—52	Single deck comb.	1899	Milnes	28	Peckham Cantilever	BTH GE52 2 x 25hp	BTH B13
53—58	Single deck	1900	ER&TCW	28	Brill 21E	BTH GE58 2 x 35hp	BTH B13
59—73	Open top	1900	ER&TCW	22/29	Peckham Cantilever	BTH GE52 2 x 25hp	BTH B13
74—88	Open top	1900	ER&TCW	22/29	Brill 21E	BTH GE52 2 x 25hp	BTH B13
89—103	Single deck	1900	Brush	28	Brill 21E	BTH GE58 2 x 35hp	BTH B13
104—123	Open top	1900-1	Brush	22/29	Brill 21E	BTH GE52 2 x 25hp	BTH B13
124—129	Single deck	1901	SCT	28	Brill 21E	BTH GE58 2 x 35hp	BTH B13
130	Water car	1901	SCT	—	Brill 21E	BTH GE58 2 x 35hp	BTH B13
131—155	Open top	1901	Milnes	22/29	Brill 21E	BTH GE58 2 x 35hp	BTH B13
156—165	Single deck	1902	Cravens	28	Brill 21E	BTH GE52 2 x 25hp	BTH B13
166	Works car (ex 15)	(1874) elec. 1902	Starbuck ex-horse	—	Brill 21E	BTH GE58 2 x 35hp	BTH B13
167—186	Open top	1902	Cravens	22/29	Brill 21E	BTH GE58 2 x 35hp	BTH B13
187—192	Single deck	1903	Milnes	28	Milnes	BTH GE58 2 x 35hp	BTH B13
193—198	Open top	1903	SCT	22/29	Milnes	BTH GE58 2 x 35hp	BTH B13
199	Stores car	(1877) elec. 1903	? (ex-horse)	—	?	BTH GE58 2 x 35hp	BTH
200—211	Single deck	1903	SCT	28	Brill 21E	BTH GE52 2 x 25hp	BTH B13
212	Water car	1904	SCT	—	Milnes	BTH GE58 2 x 35hp	BTH B13
213—218	Open top	1904	SCT	22/29	Milnes	BTH GE58 2 x 35hp	BTH
219—243	Open top	1904	Brush	22/29	Brush A	BTH GE58 2 x 35hp	BTH
244—245	Open top	(1897) elec. 1904	Milnes ex-horse cars 6, 7	22/29	Brush A	BTH GE58 2 x 35hp	BTH
246—257	Short top cover	1905	SCT	22/30	Milnes or Brush AA	BTH GE58 2 x 35hp	BTH B13

Notes to cars 1—257 (I)

All open top cars were built without canopies. Short top covers were fitted to these cars from 1903 onwards. By 1921 all single-deck cars had been withdrawn and converted to double-deckers or snowploughs, or sold. 40 h.p. motors of types BTH RGE20 and BTH GE203 were bought from 1913 onwards to replace lower powered motors. The M. & G. Radial trucks of cars 258—272 were replaced by Peckham P22 trucks in 1917-18. There were many truck changes between the other classes of cars. Car 259 was rebuilt all-enclosed in 1911, becoming Sheffield's first enclosed-top tram. Cars 258 and 260—272 were given new enclosed top decks from 1924 onwards. Single deck cars 48, 124, 127, 156—165, 189—192, 200, 201, 205, 208 were converted to double-deckers.

Disposals

The following cars were sold in 1918-22: 41, 43, 100, 102, 126 and 206 to Barrow, 16, 35, 37, 38, 74, 176, 182, 186 to Gateshead, 56 to Glossop, 94, 140, 170, 203, 252 to Musselburgh, 58, 96, 97 to Potteries, 89, 125, 129, 187, 188, 207, 209 to Preston, 40, 44, 45, 47, 49, 91, 93, 101, 103, 128, 204, 211 to Yorkshire Woollen District.

Sheffield Corporation Tramways (continued)

Car Numbers	Type (as built)	Year built	Builder	Seats	Truck	Motors	Controllers
258—272	Balcony	1907	UEC	22/36	M&G Radial	BTH GE58 2 x 35hp	BTH B13
273—280	Snow-ploughs	elec. 1906	Milnes (ex-horse)	—	Peckham Cantilever	BTH GE52 2 x 25hp	BTH
281—295	Balcony	1912	SCT	22/36	Peckham	BTH RGE20 2 x 40hp	BTH B18 ?
296—345	Balcony (note j)	1913-	Brush	22/36	Peckham P22	BTH RGE20 2 x 40hp	BTH B18 ?
346—355	Balcony (note j)	1913-	SCT	22/36	Peckham P22	BTH RGE20 2 x 40hp	BTH B18 ?
366—369 (note a)	Enclosed top	Bought 1917	ER&TCW	26/36	Brill 21E	BTH GE58 2 x 35hp	BTH
Ten cars (note a)	Enclosed top	Bought 1918	ER&TCW	22/34	Brill 21E	DK 25A 2 x 25hp	DK DB1 Form D
367—369	Enclosed	1918-1921	SCT	28/48 (note c)	Peckham P22	BTH GE203 2 x 40hp	BTH
370—375	(numbers reserved for works cars; see note b)						
376—400	Enclosed	1921-1922	Brush	28/48 (note c)	Peckham P22	BTH GE203 2 x 40hp	BTH
401—450	Enclosed	1919-1920	SCT	28/48	Peckham P22	BTH GE203 2 x 40hp	BTH
451—500	Enclosed	1926-1927	Cravens	28/40	Peckham P22	MV 102D 2 x 50hp	BTH OK1B
Eight cars (note d)	Balcony	Bought 1926	ER&TCW	22/34	Brill 21E	DK 25A 2 x 25hp	DK DB1 Form D
I (II)	Enclosed straight sided	1927	Cravens	24/37	Peckham P22	MV 102 2 x 50hp	BTH B510
2—35 (II)	Enclosed straight sided	1928-1930	SCT	24/37	Peckham P22	MV 102 2 x 50hp	BTH B510
36—60 (II)	Enclosed	1924-1925	Brush	28/40	Peckham P22	BTH B503 2 x 40hp	BTH B510
61—130 (II)	Enclosed straight sided	1930-1933	SCT	24/37	Peckham P22	MV 102DR 2 x 50hp	BTH B510
131—155 (II)	Enclosed straight sided	1929-1930	Hill	24/37	Peckham P22	MV 102 2 x 50hp	BTH B510
370 (II)	Enclosed straight sided	1931	SCT	24/37	Peckham P22	MV 116Z 2 x 50hp	BTH B510
156—230 (II)	Enclosed straight sided	1933-1935	SCT	24/37	Peckham P22	MV 102DR 2 x 50hp	BTH B510
231—242 (II)	Enclosed domed roof	1936	SCT	24/37	Peckham P22	MV 102DR 2 x 50hp	BTH B510
243—248 (II)	Enclosed straight sided	1936	SCT	24/37	Peckham P22	WT 286 or MV 116 2 x 50hp	BTH B510
249—303 (II)	Enclosed domed roof	1936-1939	SCT	24/37	Peckham P22	MV 102DR 2 x 50hp	BTH B510
336—350 (II)	Enclosed (ex 258-272)	1907 (Note k)	UEC	22/36	Peckham P22	Various 2 x 40hp	BTH B510
352—365 (II)	Snow ploughs	various	various (see note f)	—	Brill 21E (car 356, Milnes)	Mostly GE 58 2 x 35hp	various

Sheffield Corporation Tramways (continued)

Car Numbers	Type (as built)	Year built	Builder	Seats	Truck	Motors	Controllers
311—324 (II)	Enclosed (by SCT)	Bought 1941 (note g)	Hurst Nelson	24/36	Brill 21E	BTH GE58 2 x 35hp	BTH B3
325—334 (II)	Enclosed (by SCT)	Bought 1943 (note h)	EE	19/40	Brill 21E	EE DK 31A 2 x 50hp	DK DB1 Form K4
14 cars (note e)	Enclosed domed roof	1941-1944	SCT	24/37	Peckham P22	MV 102DR 2 x 50hp	BTH B510
501	Jubilee	1946	SCT	26/36	M&T588	MV 102DR3 2 x 65hp	BTH B510
502—536	Jubilee	1950-1952	Roberts	26/36	M&T588	MV 102DR3 2 x 65hp	BTH B510

Building dates for post-1927 cars :

Cars 2—10 in 1928, 11—29 and 131—148 in 1929, 30—35, 61—72 and 149—155 in 1930, 73—91 in 1931, 92—121 in 1932, 122—130 and 156—170 in 1933, 171—201 in 1934, 202—230 in 1935, 231—257 in 1936, 258—279 in 1937, 280—299 in 1938, 300—303 in 1939, 501 in 1946, 502—513 in 1950, 514—531 and 533—534 in 1951, 532, 535 and 536 in 1952.

Notes

(a) Cars 356—365 (I) were built in 1903 for the London County Council (Class B), their LCC numbers were respectively 160, 116, 119, 126, 121, 156, 108, 103, 152 and 188.
Ten additional LCC B-class cars built in 1903 were bought by Sheffield in June and July 1918 and became Sheffield 56, 94, 125, 129, 187, 188, 203, 207, 209 and 210. Their respective LCC numbers were 173, 193, 166, 181, 170, 186 171, 149, 179 and 185. SCT numbers 56, 94, 125 and 129 were bodies only and were given Peckham P22 trucks and BTH equipments at Sheffield. SCT 56 and 94 were later renumbered 128 and 90 respectively.

(b) The series 371—375 was used from 1933 for water cars and stores cars formerly carrying lower numbers, 371—372 were water cars, 373—375 were ex-horse stores cars, 375 (ex 166) was originally horse car 15.

(c) Those cars which originally seated 28/48 were later reduced to 28/37 by reducing top deck seating from two-and-two to two-and-one.

(d) Eight former London County Council B-class cars built in 1903 were bought by Sheffield from Rotherham in 1926 (Rotherham 40—47). Six were used as Sheffield 91—96) (II) and two (40 and 44) were scrapped. Rotherham had converted these cars to open-balcony.

(e) Fourteen new domed-roof cars ("Blitz" class) were built to replace cars lost through enemy action. Numbers and building dates were cars 83 and 85 in 1941, cars 100, 112, 119, 129, 133, 192 and 227 in 1942, cars 201, 261 and 274 in 1943, cars 430 and 483 in 1944.

(f) Snowplough cars 352—365 were converted at various dates (1920-33) from passenger cars. The original numbers of the cars which became 352, 354 and 356—365 were respectively 172, 274, 46, 276, 185, 225, 226, 111, 113, 99, 39, 42, 73 and 77. Cars 353 and 355 were formerly ex-horse snowploughs 274 and 276.

(g) Cars 311—324 (II) were ex Newcastle 122, 124, 113, 129, 118, 117, 114, 116, 112, 119, 125, 126, 123 and 128, built by Hurst Nelson & Co. in 1901.

(h) Cars 325—334 (II) were ex Bradford 214, 243, 242, 216, 237, 251, 257, 215, 219, and 217, built by English Electric in 1920-21. Car 330 became a rail grinder in 1951.

(j) Cars 290, 296—349, 351, 354 and 355 of 1912-14 were given new enclosed top decks from 1924 onwards.

(k) Cars 258—272 of 1907 were renumbered 336—350 in 1937. Car 349 became a stores car in 1951, car 350 became a snowplough in 1953.

General notes

In the classes of car with 50 h.p. motors, a few cars had GEC WT286JL or MV 116 50 h.p. motors instead of the standard MV 102 or MV 102DR type. Eight cars later received MV 102DR3 65 h.p. motors; in 1956, these were in cars 160, 212, 252, 254, 265, 283, 290 and 301. Some cars which originally had GE203 40 h.p. motors were later re-equipped with MV 102 or BTH 503 50 h.p. motors, mainly in series 376—450. Car 370 (II) had aluminium bodywork. The Peckham P22 trucks were built by Brush, except for the last 25 which were by EMB. Cars from 203 onwards received a modern mainly cream livery as new, in place of the dark blue and cream with gold lining and numerals which was retained for many of the older cars.

Key to Abbreviations and Manufacturers :

BEC — The British Electric Car Company Ltd., Trafford Park, Manchester.
Brill — The J. G. Brill Company, Philadelphia, USA.
BTH — The British Thomson-Houston Co. Ltd., Rugby.
Brush — The Brush Electrical Engineering Co. Ltd., Loughborough.
Cravens — Cravens Railway Carriage & Wagon Co. Ltd., Darnall, Sheffield.
CP — Crompton Parkinson & Co. Ltd., Traction Division, Chelmsford.
DK — Dick, Kerr & Co. Ltd., Preston.
EE — The English Electric Co. Ltd., Preston.
EMB — The Electro-Mechanical Brake Co. Ltd., West Bromwich.
ER&TCW — The Electric Railway & Tramway Carriage Works Ltd., Preston.
Falkenried — Waggonfabrik Falkenried, Hamburg, Germany.
GE — The General Electric Company, Schenectady, USA.
GEC — General Electric Co. Ltd., Witton Works, Birmingham.
G&DT — Gateshead & District Tramways Co. Ltd., Gateshead.
GCR — Great Central Railway Company.
GGST — Great Grimsby Street Tramways Company.
Hill — W. & E. Hill Ltd., Boatbuilders, South Shields.
HCT — Hull City Tramways, Liverpool Road Works.
Hurst Nelson — Hurst Nelson & Co. Ltd., Motherwell, Scotland.
LCT — Leeds City Tramways, Kirkstall Road Car Works.
Milnes — Geo. F. Milnes & Co. Ltd., Birkenhead (subsequently at Hadley, Shropshire).
Milnes Voss — G. C. Milnes, Voss & Co. Ltd., Birkenhead.
M & G — Mountain & Gibson Ltd., Bury, Lancs.
M & T — Maley and Taunton Ltd., Wednesbury.
MSCC — Malleable Steel Castings Co. Ltd., Wigan.
MV — The Metropolitan-Vickers Electrical Co. Ltd., Trafford Park, Manchester (successors to Westinghouse).
Peckham - Trucks built by or for the Peckham Truck & Engineering Co. Ltd. Most post-1908 Peckham trucks were built by the Brush Electrical Engineering Co. Ltd.
Raworth — Raworth's Traction Patents Ltd.
Roberts — Charles Roberts & Co. Ltd., Horbury Junction, near Wakefield.
Siemens — Siemens Brothers Dynamo Works Ltd., Stafford.
SCT — Sheffield City Tramways, Queens Road Works.
Starbuck — Starbuck Car & Wagon Co. Ltd., Birkenhead.
UEC — United Electric Car Company Ltd., Preston.
Westinghouse — Westinghouse Electric Co. Ltd., Trafford Park.

The Electric Railway & Tramway Carriage Works Ltd. (renamed United Electric Car Company Ltd. from 25 September 1905) was a subsidiary of Dick, Kerr & Co. Ltd., which merged with other electrical companies on 14 December 1918 to form The English Electric Company Ltd.

Doncaster Corporation 12 on the Racecourse route in Bennetthorpe.
(courtesy T.M.S.

Doncaster's first 25 trams were built at Preston in 1902-3 and were 56-seat four-wheelers with open top decks. During the St. Leger race meetings at Town Moor these small cars would carry up to 150 passengers, running non-stop from the town centre to the Racecourse terminus.

(*courtesy T.M.S.*

Most of Doncaster's original trams had been fitted with top covers by 1913. In this picture No. 6 is standing at the town terminus of the Beckett Road route in St. Sepulchre Gate.

(*courtesy T.M.S.*

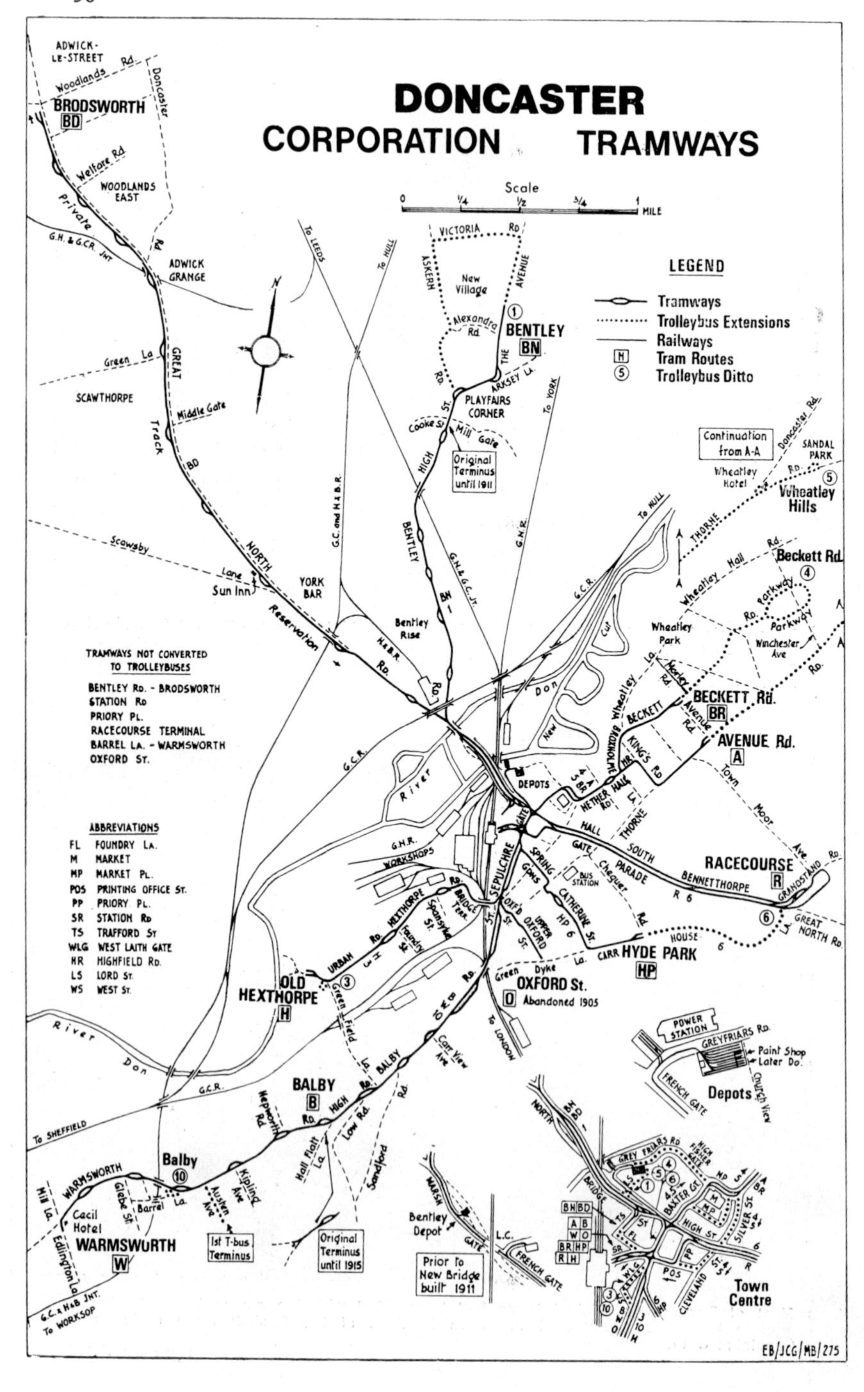
DONCASTER
CORPORATION TRAMWAYS
Scale
0 1/4 1/2 3/4 1 MILE
LEGEND
Tramways
Trolleybus Extensions
Railways
H Tram Routes
5 Trolleybus Ditto
TRAMWAYS NOT CONVERTED TO TROLLEYBUSES
BENTLEY Rd. - BRODSWORTH
STATION Rd
PRIORY PL.
RACECOURSE TERMINAL
BARREL LA. - WARMSWORTH
OXFORD St.
ABBREVIATIONS
FL FOUNDRY LA.
M MARKET
MP MARKET PL.
POS PRINTING OFFICE ST.
PP PRIORY PL.
SR STATION Rd
TS TRAFFORD St
WLG WEST LAITH GATE
HR HIGHFIELD Rd.
LS LORD St.
WS WEST St.
ADWICK-LE-STREET
BRODSWORTH BD
WOODLANDS EAST
ADWICK GRANGE
SCAWTHORPE
Sun Inn
YORK BAR
BENTLEY BN
PLAYFAIRS CORNER
Original Terminus until 1911
New Village
Continuation from A-A
Wheatley Hotel
SANDAL PARK
Wheatley Hills
Beckett Rd.
BECKETT Rd. BR
AVENUE Rd. A
DEPOTS
RACECOURSE R
HYDE PARK HP
OXFORD St. O
Abandoned 1905
OLD HEXTHORPE H
BALBY B
Balby 10
WARMSWORTH W
Cecil Hotel
1st T-bus Terminus
Original Terminus until 1915
Bentley Depot
Prior to New Bridge built 1911
POWER STATION
GREYFRIARS Rd.
Paint Shop Later Do.
Depots
Town Centre
To SHEFFIELD
To WORKSOP
To LONDON
To LEEDS
To HULL
To YORK
EB/JCG/MB/275

Doncaster's trams ran on an unusual type of rail, with the groove in the centre. These three cars are at St. James' Church, the junction of the routes to Hexthorpe, Balby and Oxford Street.
(courtesy G. L. Gundry

Doncaster Corporation 34 waiting on the depot approach line in 1933.
(M. J. O'Connor

The last ten Doncaster trams were built in 1920 and were used mainly on the long reserved-track route to Brodsworth.
(M. J. O'Connor

HULL TRAMWAYS

Horse tramways operated in Hull from 1875 to 1901, with services to Beverley Road, Spring Bank, Hessle Road, Holderness Road, Anlaby Road and Victoria Pier. This photograph was taken at the Temple Street depot.
(T.M.S.

The service along Hedon Road to the Alexandra Dock was provided by the Drypool and Marfleet Steam Tramways Company Ltd., with Thomas Green engines and Milnes bogie trailers.
(T.M.S.

The first Hull electric tramways, from St. John Street to Anlaby Road and Hessle Road, were opened on July 5, 1899.
(T.M.S.

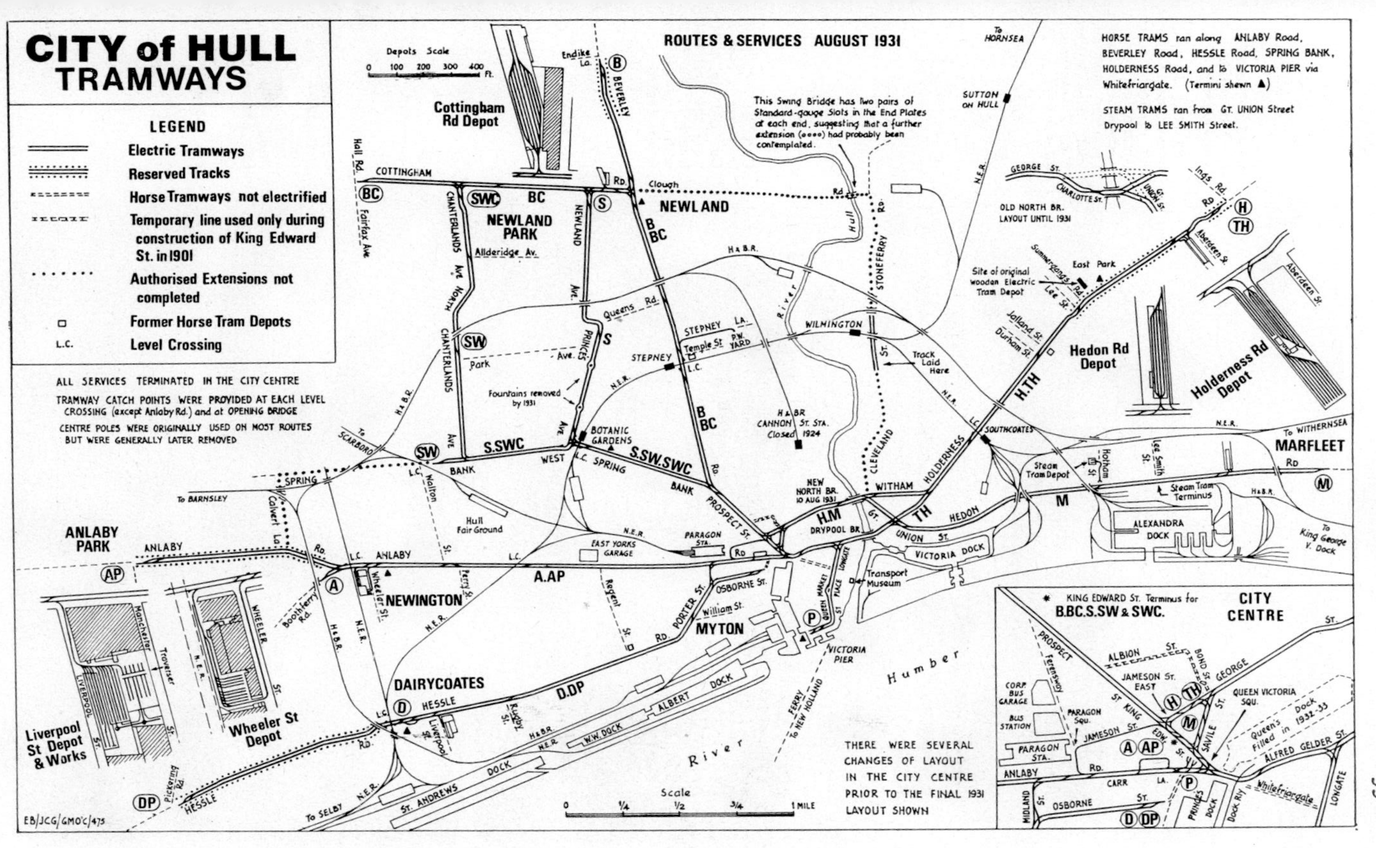
CITY of HULL
TRAMWAYS
LEGEND
Electric Tramways
Reserved Tracks
Horse Tramways not electrified
Temporary line used only during construction of King Edward St. in 1901
Authorised Extensions not completed
Former Horse Tram Depots
L.C. Level Crossing
ALL SERVICES TERMINATED IN THE CITY CENTRE
TRAMWAY CATCH POINTS WERE PROVIDED AT EACH LEVEL CROSSING (except Anlaby Rd.) and at OPENING BRIDGE
CENTRE POLES WERE ORIGINALLY USED ON MOST ROUTES BUT WERE GENERALLY LATER REMOVED
ROUTES & SERVICES AUGUST 1931
Depots Scale 0 100 200 300 400 Ft.
Cottingham Rd Depot
This Swing Bridge has two pairs of Standard-gauge Slots in the End Plates of each end, suggesting that a further extension (oooo) had probably been contemplated.
HORSE TRAMS ran along ANLABY Road, BEVERLEY Road, HESSLE Road, SPRING BANK, HOLDERNESS Road, and to VICTORIA PIER via Whitefriargate. (Termini shewn ▲)
STEAM TRAMS ran from GT. UNION Street Drypool to LEE SMITH Street.
OLD NORTH BR. LAYOUT UNTIL 1931
Site of original wooden Electric Tram Depot
Hedon Rd Depot
Holderness Rd Depot
NEWLAND
NEWLAND PARK
MARFLEET
NEWINGTON
DAIRYCOATES
MYTON
ANLABY PARK
H&BR CANNON St. STA. Closed 1924
NEW NORTH BR. 10 AUG 1931
Fountains removed by 1931
Track Laid Here
Steam Tram Depot
Steam Tram Terminus
Transport Museum
VICTORIA PIER
FERRY to NEW HOLLAND
Humber
River
Liverpool St Depot & Works
Wheeler St Depot
* KING EDWARD St. Terminus for B.BC.S.SW & SWC.
CITY CENTRE
Queen's Dock Filled in 1932-33
THERE WERE SEVERAL CHANGES OF LAYOUT IN THE CITY CENTRE PRIOR TO THE FINAL 1931 LAYOUT SHOWN
Scale 0 1/4 1/2 3/4 1 MILE
EB/JCG/GMO'C/475

DEVELOPMENT OF THE HULL TRAMCAR

The first 60 Hull trams, and 25 similar trailers, were uncanopied 51-seat 4-wheel cars built in 1898, 1899 and 1900. The trailers were motorised after a year.
(Tramway & Railway World

Cars 91-100, built by Hurst Nelson & Co. Ltd. in 1901, were the first Hull trams to be built with full - length upper decks.
(T.M.S.

Cars 102-116 of 1903 were designed as open-top vehicles but were fitted with short top covers before entering service. This view shows cor 108 at Victoria Square.
(courtesy G. L. Gundry

DEVELOPMENT OF THE HULL TRAMCAR

Between 1903 and 1909 the first 100 Hull trams were fitted with this and similar types of top cover. No. 2 of the original batch is shown here at Wheeler Street terminus on Anlaby Road.

The last new Hull trams, 161 to 180, were delivered in 1915 and had covered balconies. No. 172 is seen here outside Liverpool Street works in May, 1938. The previous batches (117-136 and 137-160) were similar except that the roof did not extend over the balconies.
(W. A. Camwell

Between 1921 and 1933, most Hull trams were rebuilt with enclosed tcp decks. No. 134 is seen here on May 22, 1938. outside Liverpool Street works at Dairycoates, where it was built and later rebuilt.
(W. A. Camwell

Hull No. 114 at Beverley Road terminus (Endike Lane) on March 27, 1937.
(H. B. Priestley M.A., block courtesy T.M.S.

Hull No. 160 at Holderness Road terminus on July 7, 1937. Four Hull tram routes included sections of reserved track.
(H. B. Priestley, M.A., block courtesy T.M.S.

In addition to the many four-wheel cars, Hull bought one bogie car in 1900 (No. 101) but resold it in 1916 to Erith Urban District Council, who used it until 1933. It was withdrawn in 1934 as London Transport 19D.

(D. W. K. Jones

Below: **Hull 20 and 163 at the Boothferry Road terminus of the Anlaby Road service on July 7, 1937.**

(H. B. Priestley M.A., block courtesy T.M.S.

GRIMSBY AND IMMINGHAM ELECTRIC RAILWAY

Above: Car No. 2 when new, photographed in 1911 at the builder's works at Loughborough.

(*Brush Electrical Engineering Co. Ltd.*

Below: The Grimsby and Immingham cars spent their entire lives out of doors, except for visits to the small three-car workshop seen on the left. In this scene at Pyewipe depot, Grimsby, on July 17, 1938, car No. 14 (centre) is standing over the inspection pit.

(*W. A. Camwell.*

GRIMSBY AND IMMINGHAM ELECTRIC RAILWAY

In addition to the twelve long cars of the type shown on the facing page, three other types of car ran on the Grimsby and Immingham line. There were four short cars (5-8) of which No. 5, shown above, survived until 1955 as a works car. In 1948 three cars were bought from Newcastle - upon - Tyne Corporation and numbered 6, 7 and 8 (centre) and in 1951 eighteen cars were bought from the Gateshead and District Tramways Company. The lower picture shows Gateshead 18 on an engineers' wagon at Spalding, en route for Grimsby in 1951.

(R. B. Parr,
R. R. Clark,
R. S. McNaught

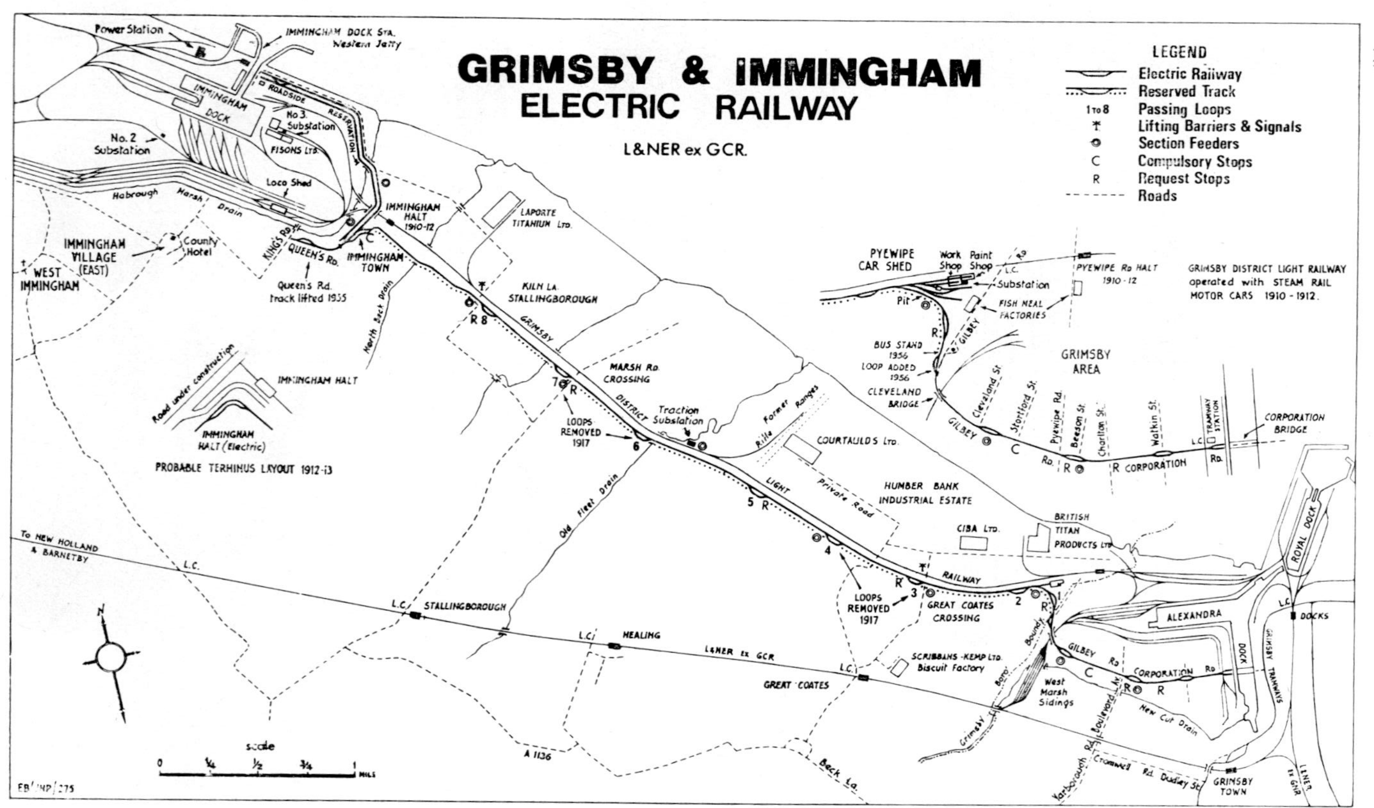
GRIMSBY & IMMINGHAM
ELECTRIC RAILWAY
L&NER ex GCR.
LEGEND
Electric Railway
Reserved Track
1 to 8 Passing Loops
Lifting Barriers & Signals
Section Feeders
C Compulsory Stops
R Request Stops
Roads
Power Station
IMMINGHAM DOCK STA.
Western Jetty
IMMINGHAM DOCK
ROADSIDE RESERVATION
No. 3 Substation
FISONS LTD.
No. 2 Substation
Loco Shed
Habrough Marsh Drain
IMMINGHAM HALT 1910-12
KING'S Rd.
QUEEN'S Rd.
IMMINGHAM TOWN
Queen's Rd. track lifted 1955
IMMINGHAM VILLAGE (EAST)
County Hotel
WEST IMMINGHAM
LAPORTE TITANIUM LTD.
KILN LA. STALLINGBOROUGH
North Beck Drain
GRIMSBY
DISTRICT
LIGHT
RAILWAY
MARSH RD. CROSSING
LOOPS REMOVED 1917
Traction Substation
Rifle Former Ranges
COURTAULDS LTD.
Private Road
HUMBER BANK INDUSTRIAL ESTATE
CIBA LTD.
BRITISH TITAN PRODUCTS LTD.
GREAT COATES CROSSING
SCRIBBANS-KEMP LTD. Biscuit Factory
Road under construction
IMMINGHAM HALT
IMMINGHAM HALT (Electric)
PROBABLE TERMINUS LAYOUT 1912-13
Old Fleet Drain
PYEWIPE CAR SHED
Work Shop
Paint Shop
L.C.
Substation
PYEWIPE RD HALT 1910-12
FISH MEAL FACTORIES
Pit
GILBEY
BUS STAND 1956
LOOP ADDED 1956
CLEVELAND BRIDGE
GRIMSBY AREA
Cleveland St.
Stortford St.
Pyewipe Rd.
Beeson St.
Charlton St.
Watkin St.
TRAMWAY STATION
CORPORATION BRIDGE
CORPORATION Rd.
GRIMSBY DISTRICT LIGHT RAILWAY operated with STEAM RAIL MOTOR CARS 1910-1912.
To NEW HOLLAND & BARNETBY
L.C.
STALLINGBOROUGH
HEALING
L&NER ex GCR
GREAT COATES
A 1136
Beck La.
Boundy
Grimsby Boro'
West Marsh Sidings
GILBEY Rd.
CORPORATION Rd.
New Cut Drain
ALEXANDRA DOCK
ROYAL DOCK
DOCKS
GRIMSBY TRAMWAYS
Yarborough Rd.
Boulevard Av.
Cromwell Rd.
Dudley St.
GRIMSBY TOWN
L&NER ex GNR
scale
0 1/4 1/2 3/4 1 MILE
EB/IMP/275

Grimsby and Immingham car No. 12 at the Tramway Station at Corporation Bridge, Grimsby, on July 17, 1938. The lifting bridge in the background was designed to carry tram tracks, but they were never laid.

(*W. A. Camwell*

The other end of the Grimsby and Immingham line was at Immingham Dock (Easter Jetty). The right-hand track was used during the day to store the extra cars used at rush hours.

(*R. Brook*

Two views along the Grimsby and Immingham Electric Railway: ex-Gateshead car 33 near Oldfleet Drain, and ex-Great Central car No. 1 in the Dock Estate at Immingham.
(D. Tate, blocks courtesy Modern Transport

From July 1, 1956 the street-running section of the Immingham line in Grimsby was replaced by Grimsby Corporation buses, and the trams were cut back to a new terminus at Cleveland Bridge. This photograph of No. 4 also shows some of the hundreds of bicycles stored there during the day by the dock and factory workers who used the tramway.
(*J. H. Price*

One of the ex-Gateshead cars was converted to serve as a repair car, replacing the former car No. 5. This view was taken after the line closed in July, 1961.
(*J. H. Price*

YORKSHIRE
River Humber
Dock Power Station
IMMINGHAM DOCK
45
Nº3 Substation
IMMINGHAM HALT*
IMMINGHAM
Laporte Titanium Wks.
QUEENS RD
IMMINGHAM WEST
IMMINGHAM TOWN
KILN LA.
Traction Substation
Nº5 PASSING PLACE
PYEWIPE RD HALT*
PYEWIPE CAR SHED & SUBSTATION
Humber Bank
GRIMSBY
Fish Docks
STALLINGBOROUGH
HEALING
CLEVELAND BR.
NEW CLEE
GREAT COATES
GRIMSBY TOWN
GRIMSBY DOCKS
Corporation Br.
Drew Avenue
Beacon Hill Estate
CLEETHORPES

GRIMSBY & IMMINGHAM ELECTRIC RLY.
ABANDONED SECTIONS
REPLACING BUS SERVICES
" " " WORK SERVICES
BRITISH RAILWAYS, OTHER LINES
TEMPORARY STNS FOR STEAM RAIL MOTOR SERVICE 1910-12*

There is no direct road from Grimsby to Immingham, and when the electric railway closed on July 1, 1961, the replacing buses had to follow a 12-mile inland route instead of the direct 7-mile alignment of the electric line.
(*Block courtesy Modern Transport*

Great Grimsby Street Tramways

Above: **Grimsby horse tram No. 11 at the Carr Lane depot. This car was kept after electrification for use as a trailer, mainly for football traffic, and was later sold to Lincoln Corporation.**

(courtesy D. H. Yarnell)

Below: **The Board of Trade Inspector's special electric car in November, 1901, photographed at the original Cleethorpes terminus in Alexandra Road. Public service began on December 7.**

(H. Orme White, A.M.I.E.E.

Great Grimsby Street Tramways

In addition to 24 open-top cars of the type shown on the opposite page, the Great Grimsby company bought four second-hand single-deck electric cars from the former Alexandra Park Electric Railway in the North London suburbs. No. 25, seen above at Old Market Place, Grimsby, was rebuilt as an open-top double-decker, as were 26 and 28, but No. 27 was fitted in 1903 with a covered top. The lower picture shows car No. 6, one of thirteen cars rebuilt in 1908 with long open-balcony top covers.

(H. Orme White, A.M.I.E.E.

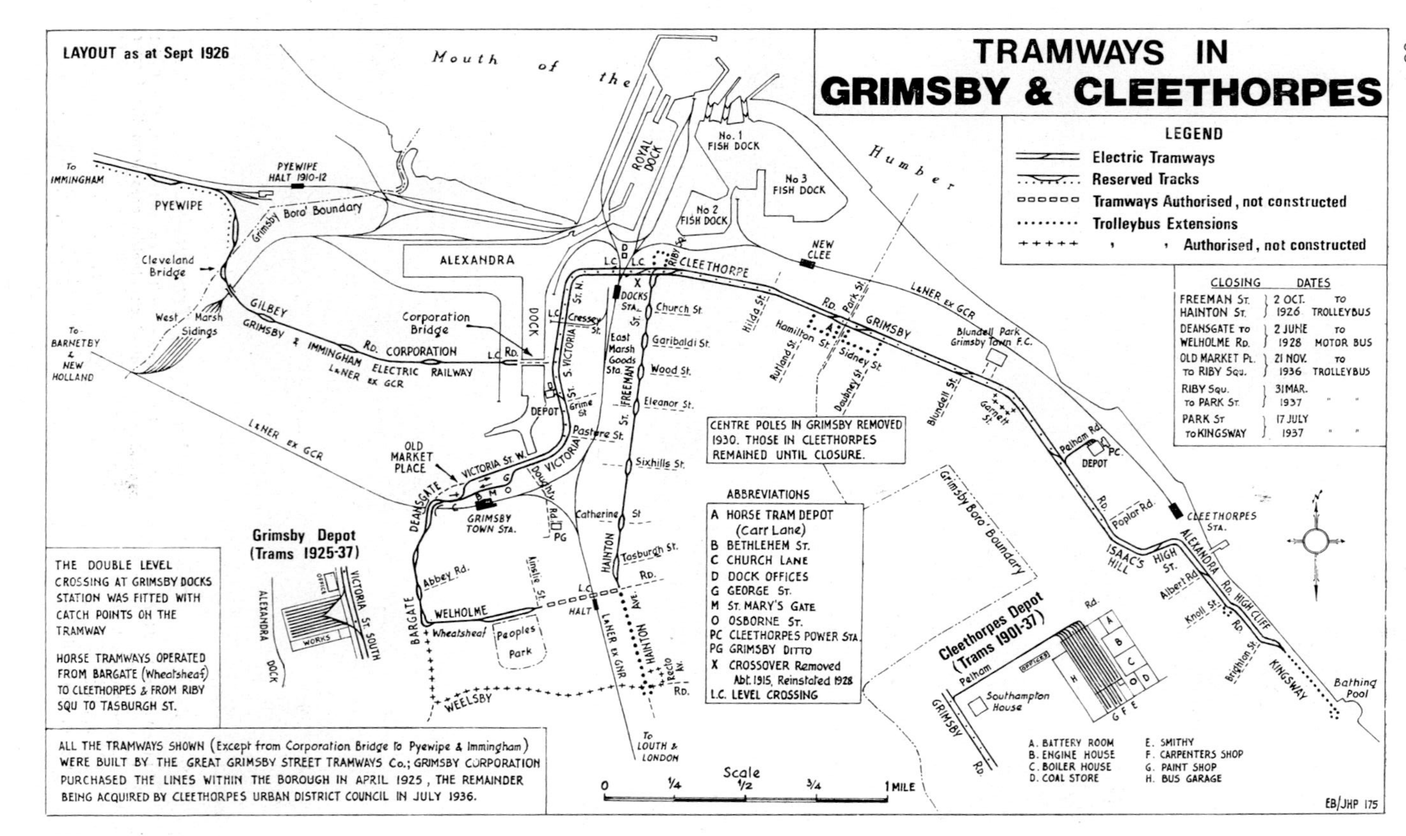
TRAMWAYS IN
GRIMSBY & CLEETHORPES
LAYOUT as at Sept 1926
LEGEND
Electric Tramways
Reserved Tracks
Tramways Authorised, not constructed
Trolleybus Extensions
" " Authorised, not constructed
CLOSING DATES
FREEMAN ST. HAINTON ST. 2 OCT. 1926 TO TROLLEYBUS
DEANSGATE TO WELHOLME RD. 2 JUNE 1928 TO MOTOR BUS
OLD MARKET PL. TO RIBY SQU. 21 NOV. 1936 TO TROLLEYBUS
RIBY SQU. TO PARK ST. 31 MAR. 1937 " "
PARK ST TO KINGSWAY 17 JULY 1937 " "
CENTRE POLES IN GRIMSBY REMOVED 1930. THOSE IN CLEETHORPES REMAINED UNTIL CLOSURE.
ABBREVIATIONS
A HORSE TRAM DEPOT (Carr Lane)
B BETHLEHEM ST.
C CHURCH LANE
D DOCK OFFICES
G GEORGE ST.
M ST. MARY'S GATE
O OSBORNE ST.
PC CLEETHORPES POWER STA.
PG GRIMSBY DITTO
X CROSSOVER Removed Abt. 1915, Reinstated 1928
L.C. LEVEL CROSSING
Mouth of the Humber
To IMMINGHAM
PYEWIPE
PYEWIPE HALT 1910-12
Grimsby Boro' Boundary
Cleveland Bridge
West Marsh Sidings
To BARNETBY & NEW HOLLAND
GILBEY
GRIMSBY & IMMINGHAM ELECTRIC RAILWAY
L&NER ex GCR
RD. CORPORATION
Corporation Bridge
ALEXANDRA
DOCK
ROYAL DOCK
No. 1 FISH DOCK
No 2 FISH DOCK
No 3 FISH DOCK
NEW CLEE
CLEETHORPE RD.
GRIMSBY
L&NER ex GCR
Blundell Park Grimsby Town F.C.
DOCKS STA.
Church St.
Garibaldi St.
Wood St.
Eleanor St.
Sixhills St.
Catherine St
Tasburgh St.
East Marsh Goods Sta.
FREEMAN ST.
HAINTON RD.
HAINTON AVE.
Recto Av.
Hilda St.
Hamilton St.
Rutland St.
Park St.
Sidney St.
Daubney St.
Blundell St.
Garnett St.
Pelham Rd.
DEPOT
Poplar Rd.
CLEETHORPES STA.
ISAAC'S HILL
HIGH ST.
ALEXANDRA RD.
HIGH CLIFF RD.
Albert Rd.
Knoll St.
Brighton St.
KINGSWAY
Bathing Pool
S. VICTORIA ST.
ST. N.
Cressey St.
Grime St
Pasture St.
VICTORIA ST. W.
Doughty Rd.
OLD MARKET PLACE
DEANSGATE
GRIMSBY TOWN STA.
Abbey Rd.
Ainslie St.
WELHOLME
BARGATE
Wheatsheaf
Peoples Park
WEELSBY
HALT
L&NER ex GNR
To LOUTH & LONDON
Grimsby Depot (Trams 1925-37)
VICTORIA ST. SOUTH
OFFICE
WORKS
ALEXANDRA DOCK
Cleethorpes Depot (Trams 1901-37)
Pelham Rd.
OFFICES
Southampton House
GRIMSBY RD.
A. BATTERY ROOM
B. ENGINE HOUSE
C. BOILER HOUSE
D. COAL STORE
E. SMITHY
F. CARPENTERS SHOP
G. PAINT SHOP
H. BUS GARAGE
Scale
0 1/4 1/2 3/4 1 MILE
EB/JHP 175
THE DOUBLE LEVEL CROSSING AT GRIMSBY DOCKS STATION WAS FITTED WITH CATCH POINTS ON THE TRAMWAY
HORSE TRAMWAYS OPERATED FROM BARGATE (Wheatsheaf) TO CLEETHORPES & FROM RIBY SQU TO TASBURGH ST.
ALL THE TRAMWAYS SHOWN (Except from Corporation Bridge to Pyewipe & Immingham) WERE BUILT BY THE GREAT GRIMSBY STREET TRAMWAYS Co.; GRIMSBY CORPORATION PURCHASED THE LINES WITHIN THE BOROUGH IN APRIL 1925, THE REMAINDER BEING ACQUIRED BY CLEETHORPES URBAN DISTRICT COUNCIL IN JULY 1936.

In 1911 the Grimsby company borrowed a model tram from the United Electric Car Company Ltd. at Preston and used it in the Coronation Trades Procession on June 22, mounted on their own motor lorry. The tram carried 25 children dressed in tramways uniform.

(H. Orme White, A.M.I.E.E.

In 1922 the Great Grimsby Street Tramways Company built a tramway touring coach and ran sixpenny trips between Cleethorpes and People's Park. After three seasons the "tram coach" was transferred to the Portsdown and Horndean Light Railway.

(H. Orme White, A.M.I.E.E.

Two of the eight cars built by the Great Grimsby Street Tramways Co. at Cleethorpes between 1925 and 1928. No. 39 (above) was fitted with a top cover after its first season of running; the other seven were built new with top covers.

(H. Orme White, A.M.I.E.E.

Grimsby Corporation took over the tramways in the borough in 1925. and bought sixteen open-balcony cars from the Sunderland District Electric Tramways for operation on the joint through service to Cleethorpes. No. 47 is seen here at Kingsway terminus in June, 1935.

(H. B. Priestley, M.A., block courtesy T.M.S.

The Great Grimsby company continued to run trams in Cleethorpes until July, 1936, when Cleethorpes Council took over. This view taken on April 24, 1937, shows two ex-Gosport open-top cars with the ex-Southport single-decker, which made the closing trip at Cleethorpes on July 17, 1937.

(H. B. Priestley M.A., block courtesy T.M.S.

THE SURVIVORS

Sheffield horse car 15 of 1874, operating along The Moor during the Christmas Shopping Festival in December, 1961. This car is preserved at Crich.
(R. J. S. Wiseman, B.A

Sheffield 330, formerly Bradford 251, was converted by Sheffield to a water car and track cleaner and now fulfils the same role at the Tramway Museum, Crich, flushing out the points before the day's service begins.
(J. H. Price

Four other Sheffield trams can be seen in operation at Crich. From left to right, they are numbers 264, 510, 46 and 189.
(J. H. Price

THE SURVIVORS

Grimsby and Immingham car 14 is owned by the Tramway Museum Society and stored by them at Clay Cross.
(*R. G. P. Tebb*

Sheffield 342 of 1907 was preserved by British Railways and transferred by them to the North-East Regional Open-Air Museum, together with Grimsby and Immingham 26, formerly Gateshead 10. The two cars are seen here in store at Consett in June, 1969.

Hull Corporation 132, photographed here at Beverley Road terminus in 1937, is preserved at Crich after spending some years operating in Leeds.
(*H. B. Priestley, M.A.*

Bibliography and Acknowledgements

The text of this book dates back to the founding of its publishers, the Light Railway Transport League, for it first appeared in print in September and October, 1938, in the League's journal *Modern Tramway* during the first year of publication. Written by Mr. W. H. Bett, it formed the fifth and sixth articles in a series with the title *Great British Tramway Networks*. These articles were later reprinted in booklet form, and were subsequently greatly expanded under the co-authorship of Mr. J. C. Gillham, retaining the *Networks* title but forming a book that has served for many years as the standard work of reference on British tramways. The fourth edition is now out of print, but individual chapters are being republished in the form of illustrated books generally similar to the present work, and four have now been issued.

The tramcar fleet lists on pages 40-48 have been compiled by J. H. Price, with the valued assistance of M. C. P. S. Bacon, G. E. Baddeley, R. Elliott, J. C. Gillham, G. M. O'Connell, M. J. O'Connor, H. B. Priestley, A. K. Terry, R. J. Wiseman and (in the past) H. Orme White, former manager of

In 1974 consultants engaged by Sheffield Corporation to report on the city's future transport suggested that tramways should be reintroduced and should be admitted to certain streets from which all other vehicles would be banned. One of the traffic-free areas will be around the Town Hall, where these three trams (Nos. 370, 12 and 515) were photographed in 1953. No. 370 was an experimental aluminium-bodied car.

P. N. Williams

the Great Grimsby Street Tramways Company. Use has also been made of Mr. C. C. Hall's recent comprehensive history of Sheffield Transport, published in 1977, and of his invaluable articles on the various South Yorkshire tramways published in *Tramway Review.* The introductory maps and those of Barnsley, Dearne District and Sheffield were drawn and (in most cases) subsequently revised by J. C. Gillham, and those of Doncaster, Grimsby, Hull, Rotherham and the Grimsby and Immingham Electric Railway were specially drawn for this book by E. Beddard from notes prepared by J. H. Price, G. E. Baddeley, M. C. P. S. Bacon and G. M. O'Connell. In certain cases full information required for the fleet lists could not be traced, and the publishers will be pleased to hear from readers who may be able to assist in completing the lists for inclusion in any further edition.

The illustrations include the best of those published previously in *Great British Tramway Networks,* to which have been added a large number that have appeared in *Modern Tramway, Trams* and *Tramway Review,* reproduced by kind permission of the respective editors. About one-third of the photographs appear for the first time, and we are most grateful to the photographers and copyright holders for permission to reproduce them, and to G. E. Baddeley and G. L. Gundry for their help in locating suitable prints. The photographs taken by the late Dr. H. A. Whitcombe are reproduced by permission of the Science Museum, South Kensington.

The publishers also record their thanks to the Board of the Tramway Museum Society for the loan of certain printing blocks used in this book. These appeared originally in *Trams,* the Society's quarterly historical journal.

Previously published references to which we have referred in compiling this book are listed below and on the following pages.

Barnsley and District Electric Traction Company Ltd.

A History of the Barnsley, Dearne, Mexborough and Rotherham Tramway Conurbation, by C. C. Hall, M.C.I.T., published in issues 51 to 58 of *Tramway Review,* 1967 to 1969.

The Tale of "Tracky", by Raymond Birch (Omnibus Society Presidential Address, 1958, dealing with history of Yorkshire Traction Co. Ltd.).

Tram and Bus Development in the West Riding, by Norman Dean (The *Omnibus Magazine,* June 1964).

Dearne District Light Railways

The references listed under Barnsley and District also contain notes on Dearne District.

Some Notes on the Dearne District Light Railway, by R. K. Kirkland, published in *Modern Tramway,* February and April 1947.

Tramway and Railway World, July 17, 1924.

The Omnibus Magazine, June 1932.

Doncaster Corporation Tramways

Doncaster Corporation Transport, 50 Years Jubilee, 1902 to 1952 (published by the Corporation).

Doncaster—The Racecourse Route, by M. C. P. S. Bacon, published in issue No. 3 of *Trams,* October 1961.

Modern Tramway, December 1944 (Fleet list).

Doncaster Transport, by C. S. Dunbar, published in *Passenger Transport,* January 1956.

Great Grimsby Street Tramways Company

The Grimsby and Cleethorpes Tramways, by W. H. Lucas, published in issue No. 10 of *Trams,* July 1963.

London's First Electric Tramway, by J. H. Price published in *The Journal of Transport History,* November 1958 (details of Alexandra Park cars).

Memories of Grimsby and Cleethorpes Transport, by W. H. Lucas (Turntable Publications, 1974).

Transport in Grimsby and Cleethorpes, by J. C. Gillham, published in *Transport World,* June 1960.

Grimsby and Immingham Electric Railway

Great Central Volume 3. by George Dow (Ian Allan, 1965).

Modern Tramway, July 1944 (article); January 1953 (car renumbering).

Modern Transport, June 4, 1961.

A history of the Grimsby and Immingham Electric Railway is being prepared for publication by Mr. J. H. Price.

Hull City Tramways

Tramway & Railway World, July 10, 1902.

Turning Losses into Profits (*Bus & Coach,* April 1939).

Passenger Transport in Hull, by G. E. Baddeley (Omnibus Society duplicated publication, 1942).

Hull's Transport Jubilee, by G. H. Pulfrey (*Transport World,* Aug. 1949).

British Bus & Tram Systems No. 19, Hull Corporation, by G. M. O'Connell, M.C.I.T. (published in *Buses Illustrated,* May-June 1957).

The Tramways of Kingston-upon-Hull, by J. S. Nicholson (published in issues 27, 28 and 29 of *Trams,* 1967-68).

British Trolleybus Systems No. 17—Hull, by G. M. O'Connell, M.C.I.T. (published in *Buses,* February and April 1973).

Fleet History of Leeds City Transport (LDTN/PSV Circle/Omnibus Society, 1969) (for details of Hull cars sold to Leeds).

Modern Transport, 23 February 1929, 18 March and 1 April 1944, 14 and 21 July 1945.

The Omnibus Magazine, September 1954.

KHCT 1899–1979; An Illustrated History of Kingston-upon-Hull City Transport (published by Kingston-upon-Hull City Transport, July 1979).